EASTER

COLORING BOOK FOR TODDLERS

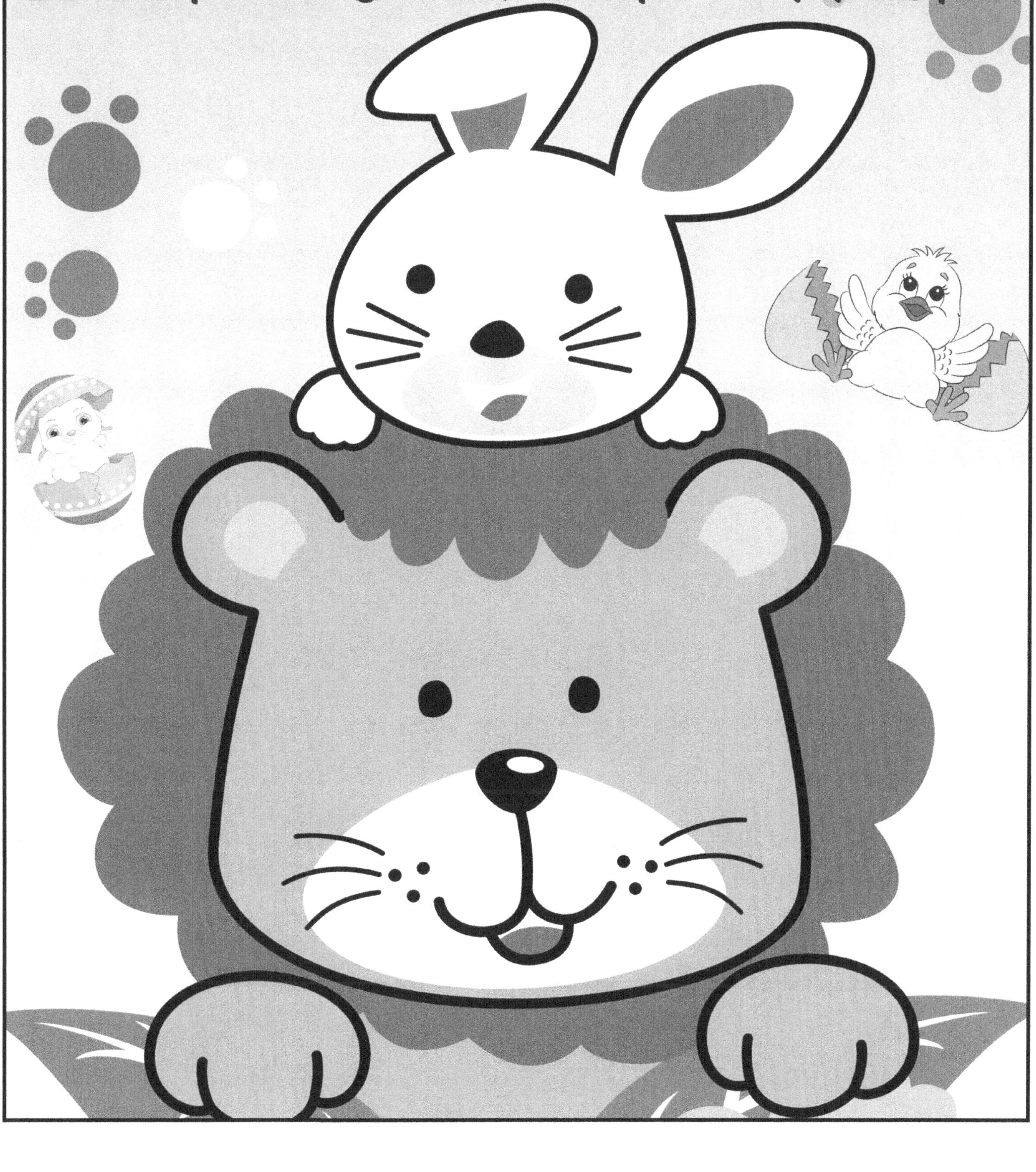

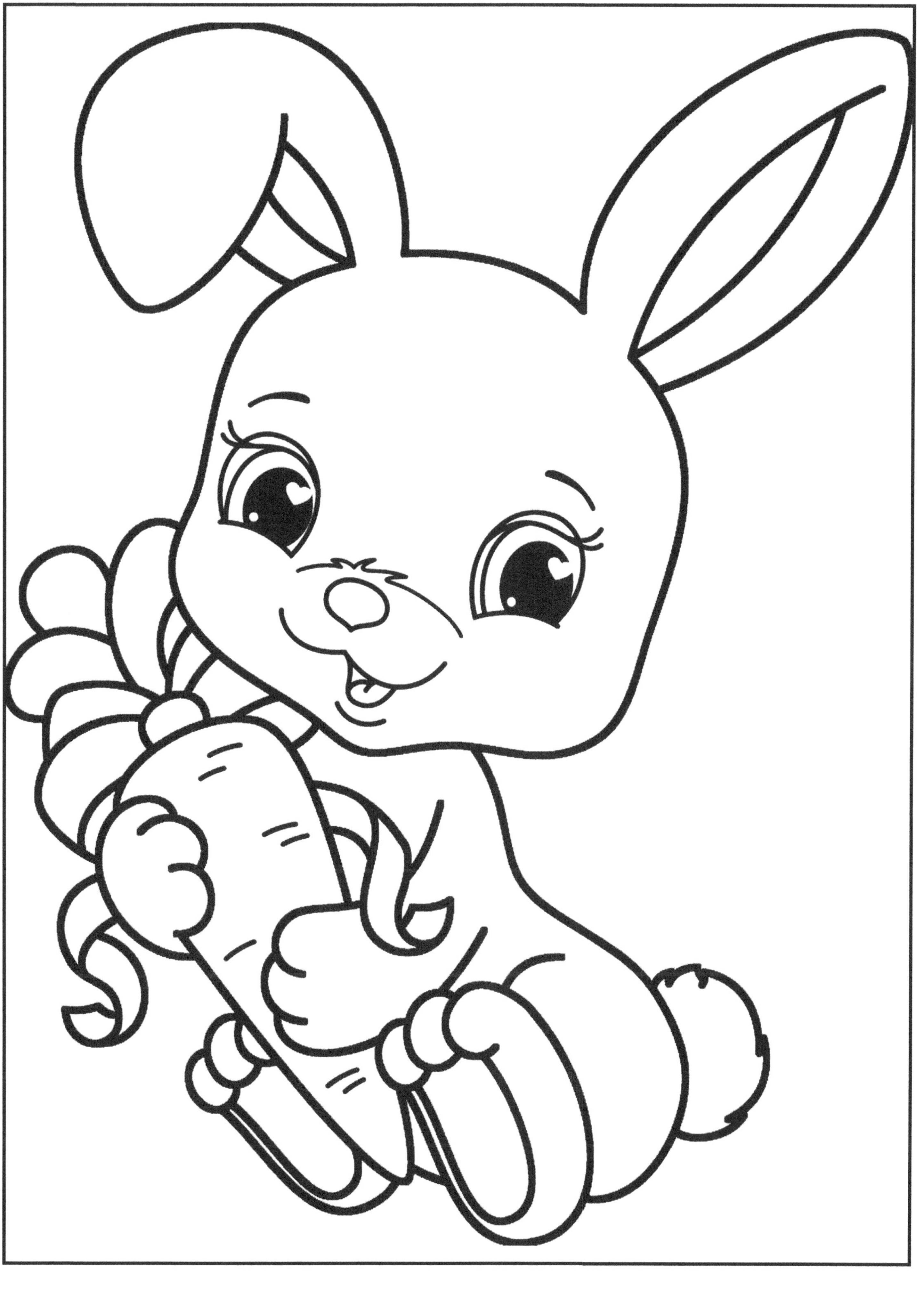

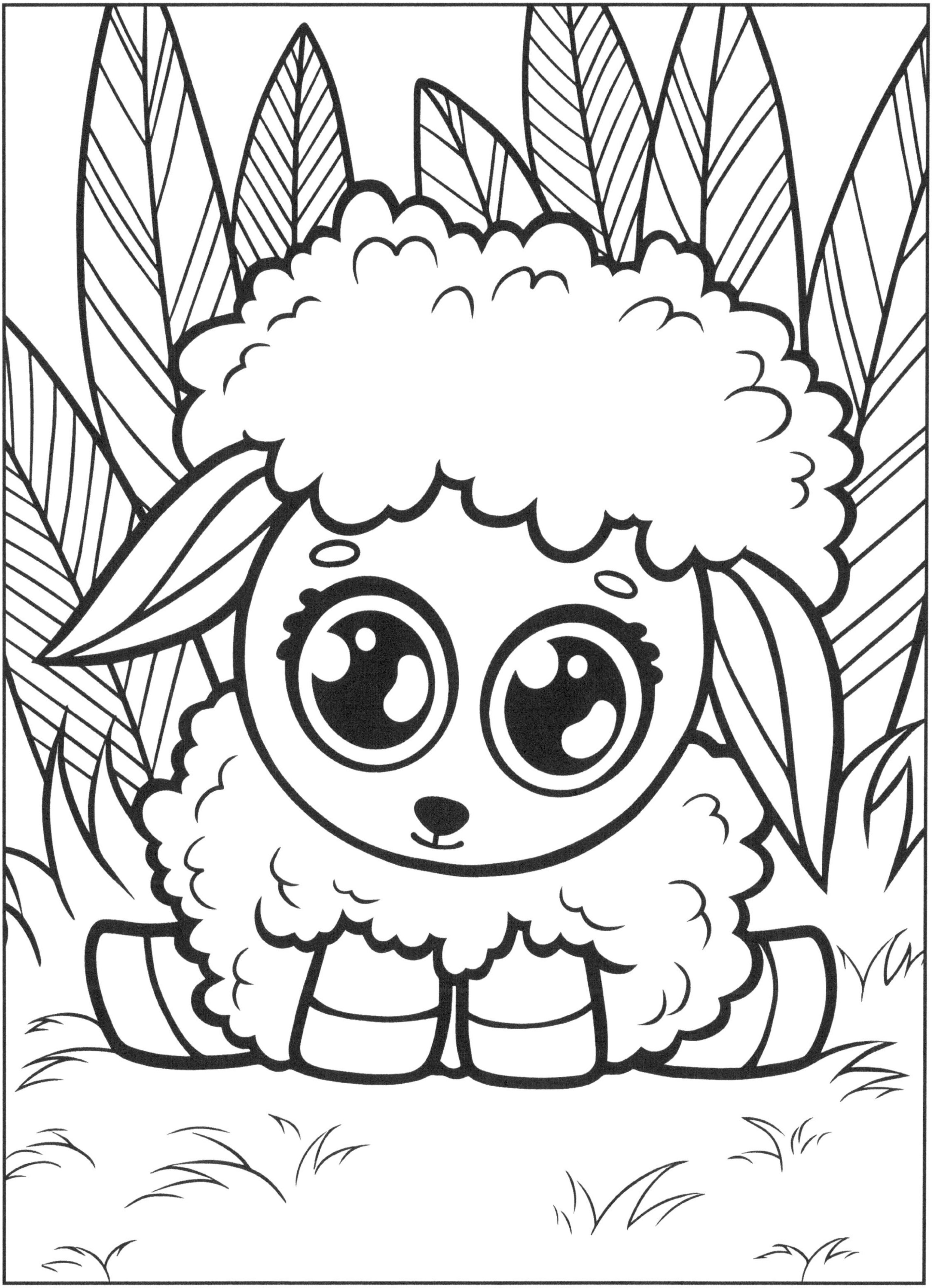

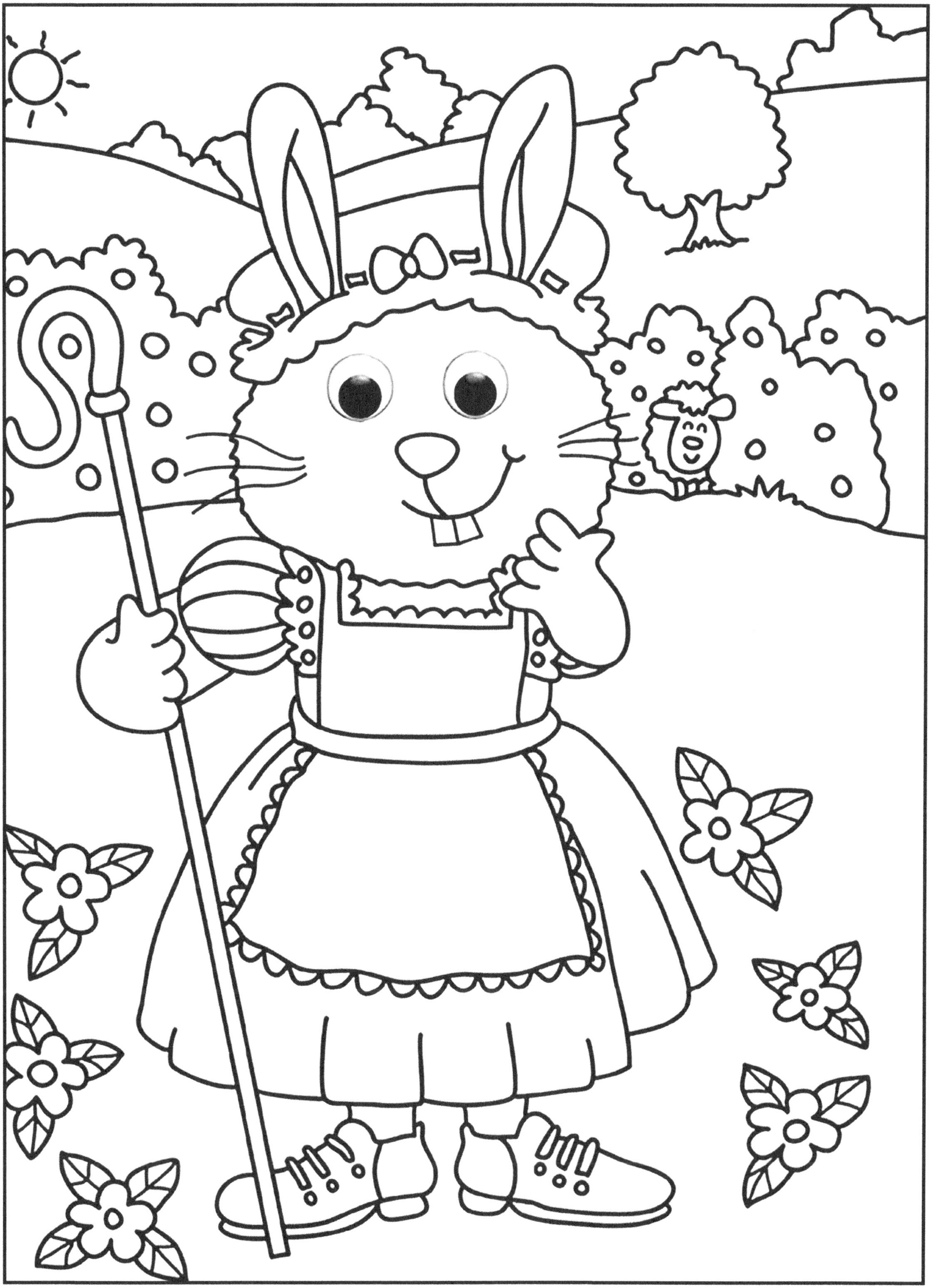

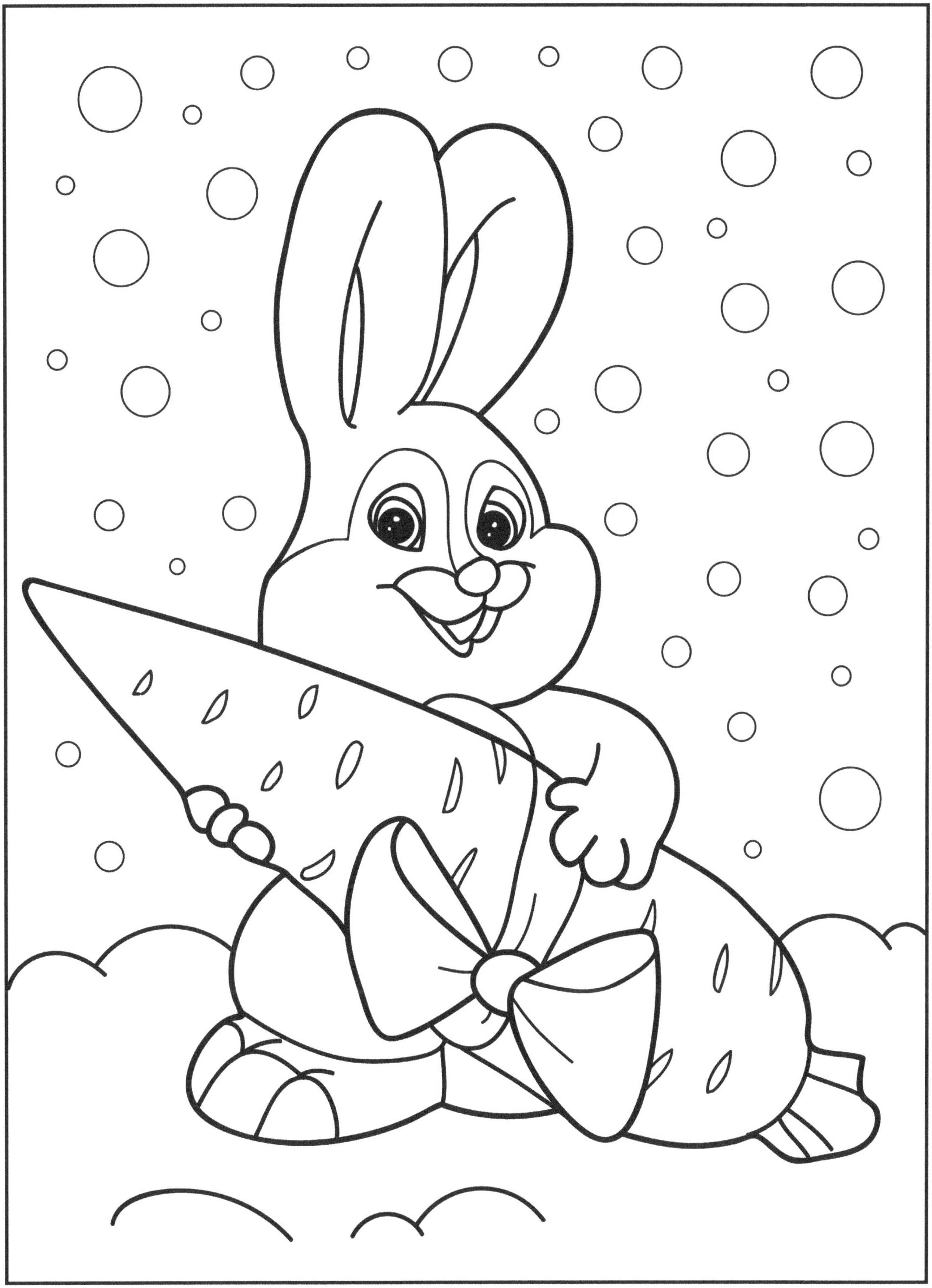

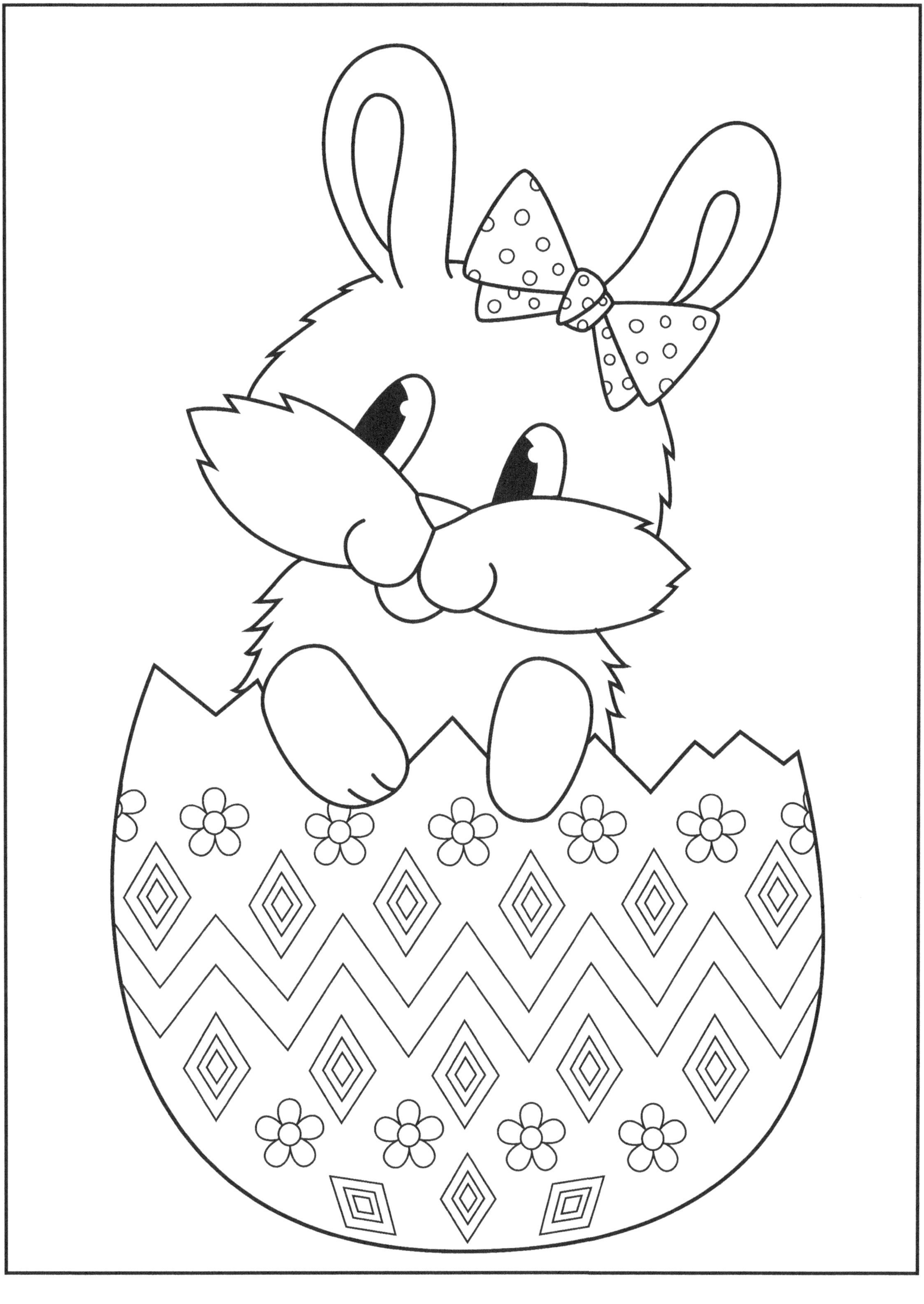

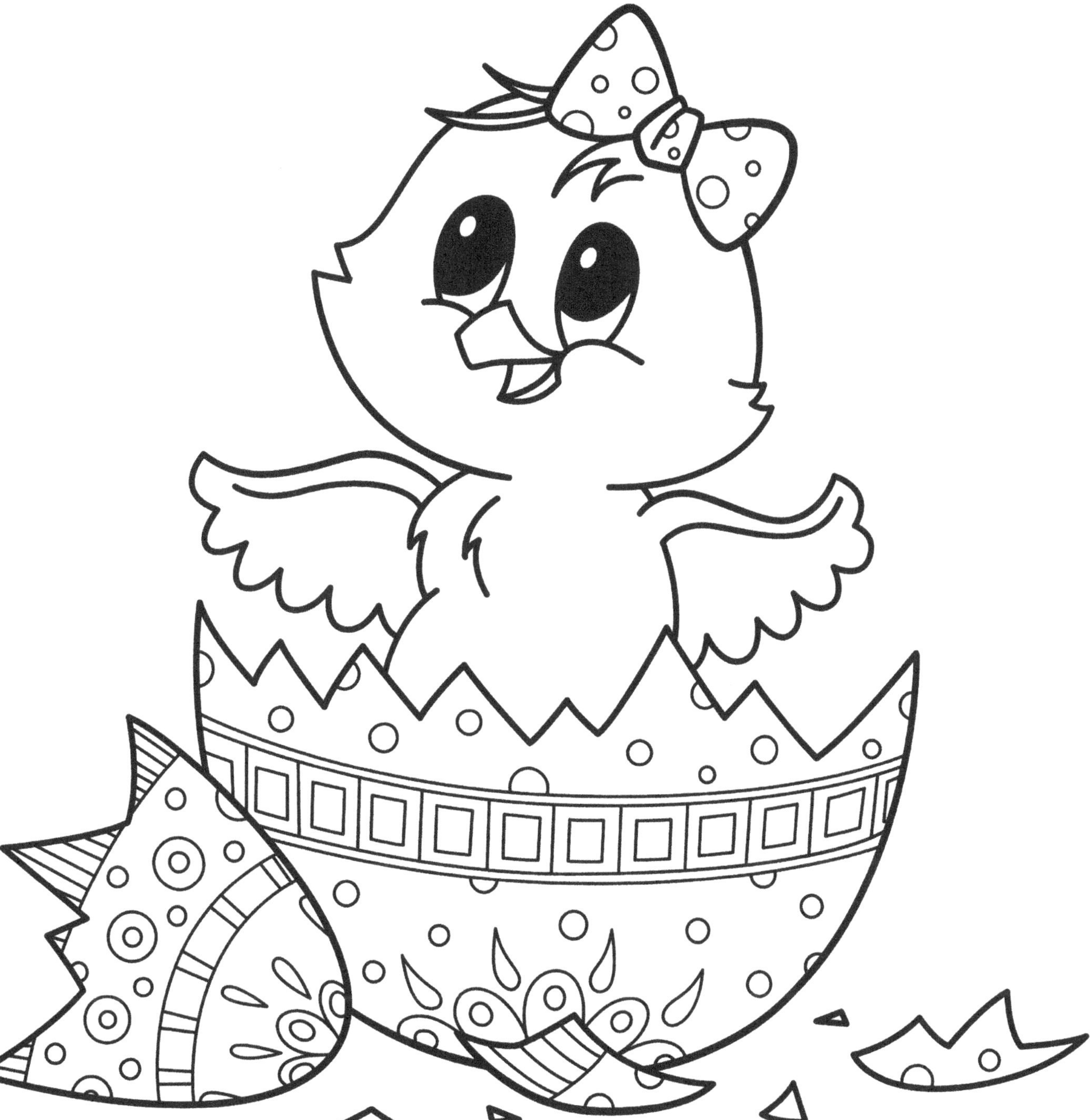

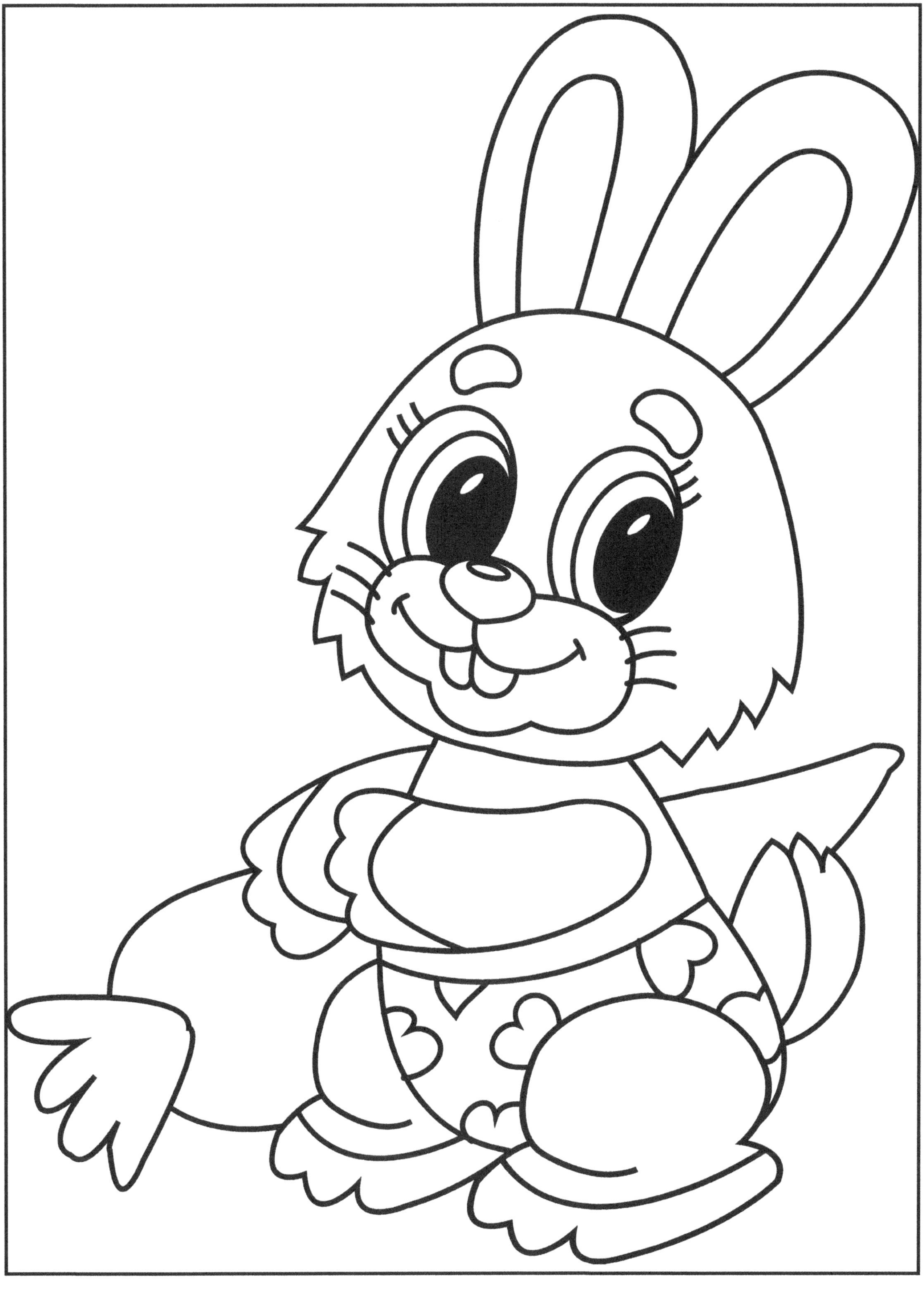

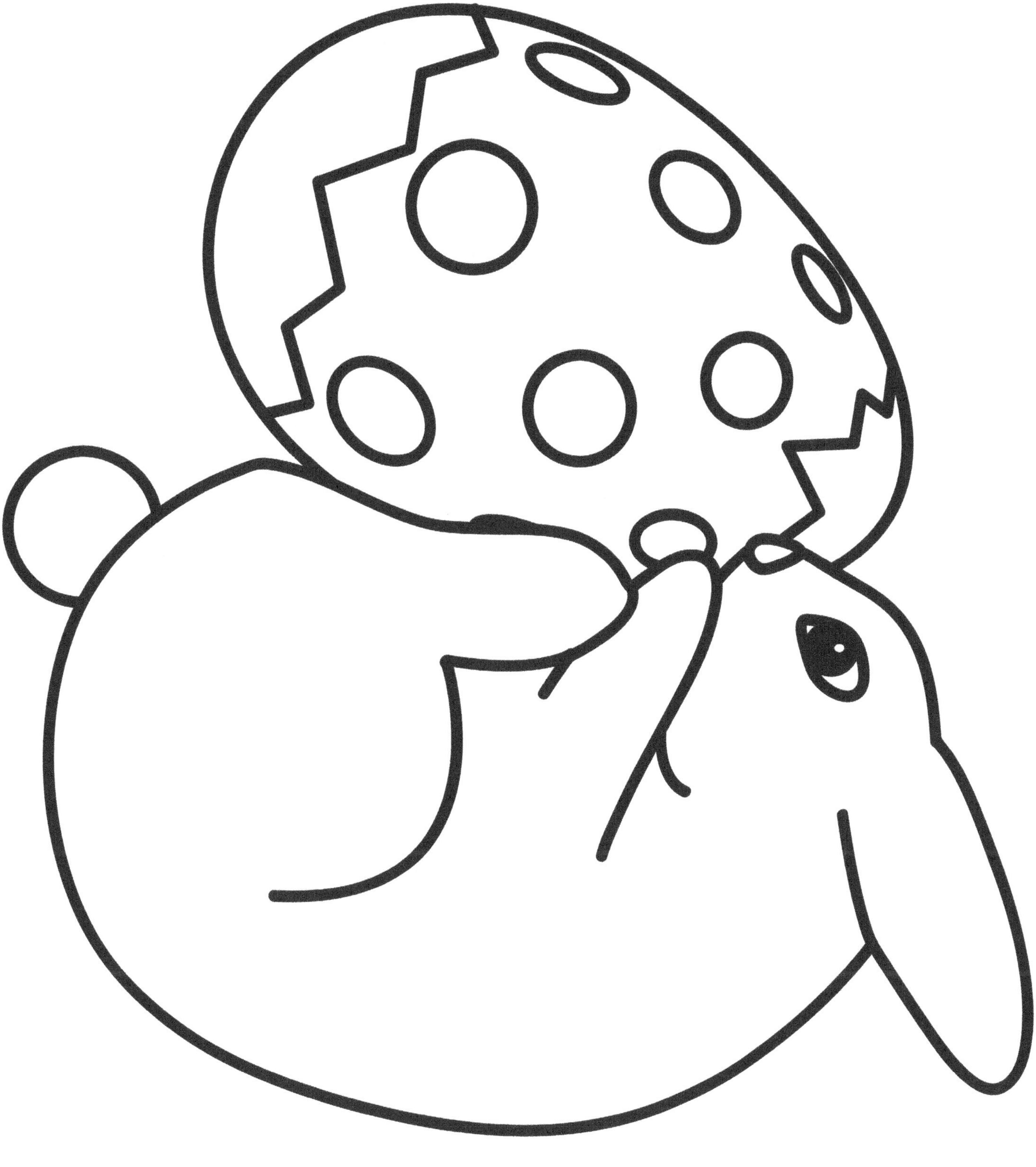

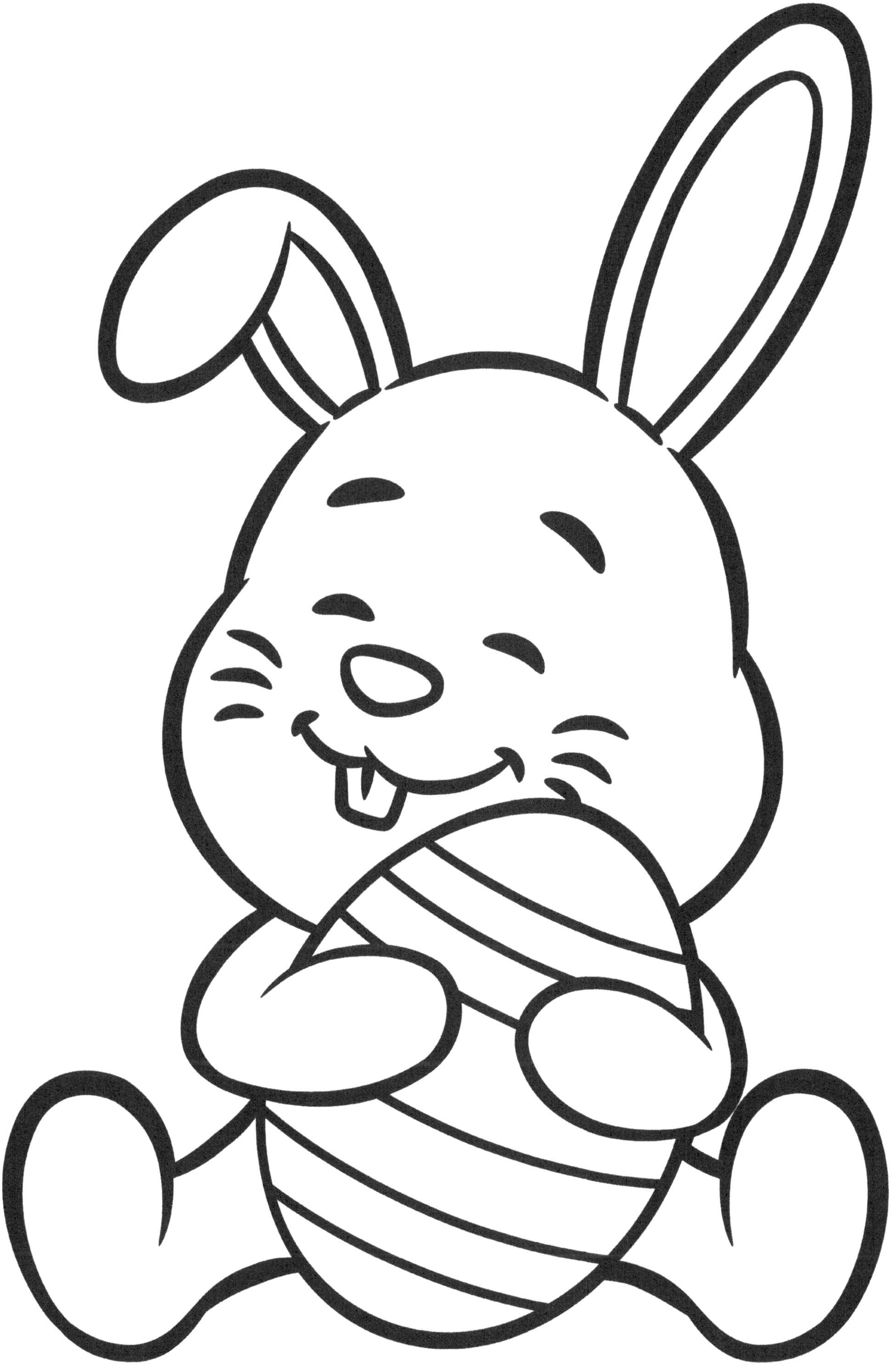

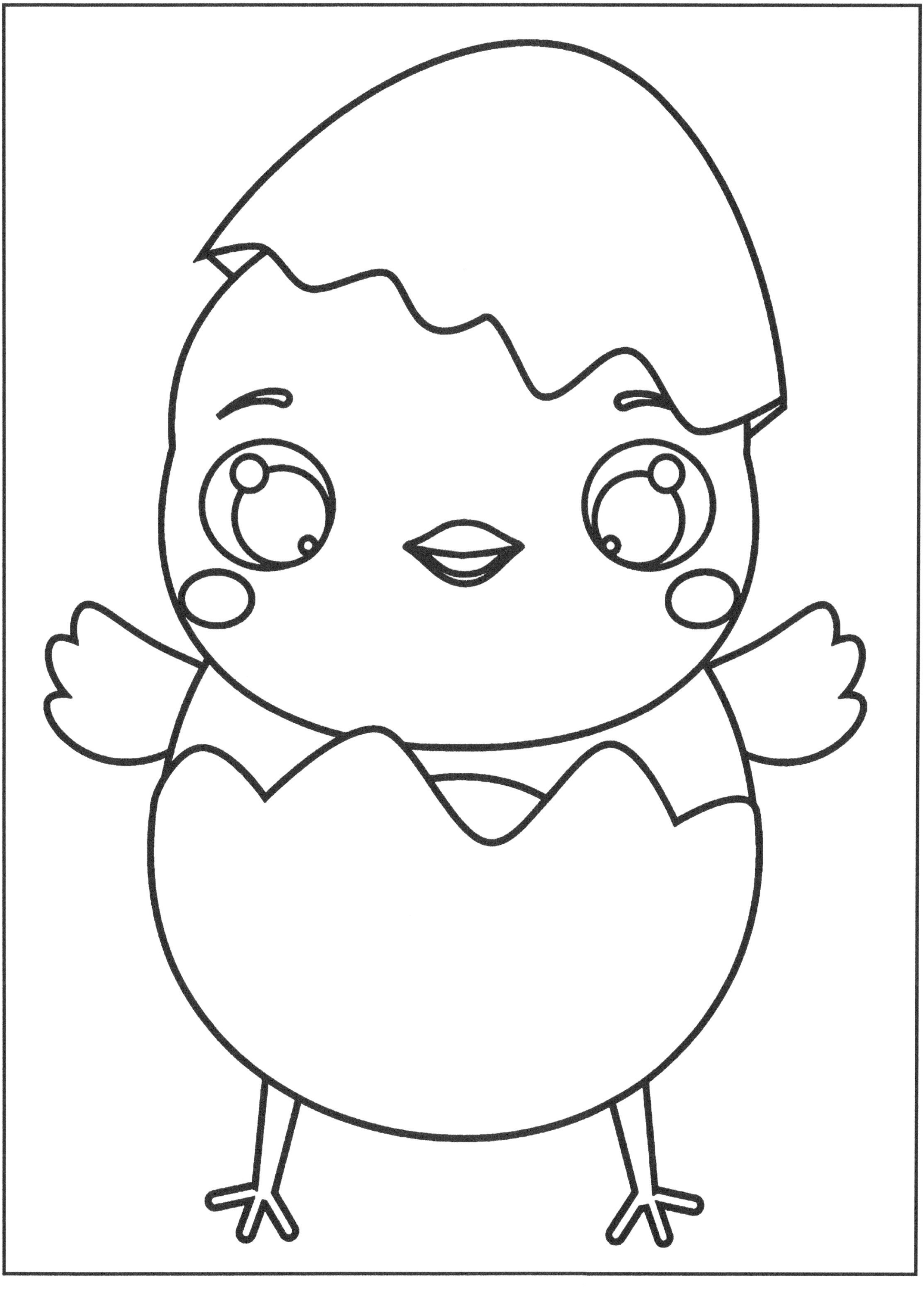

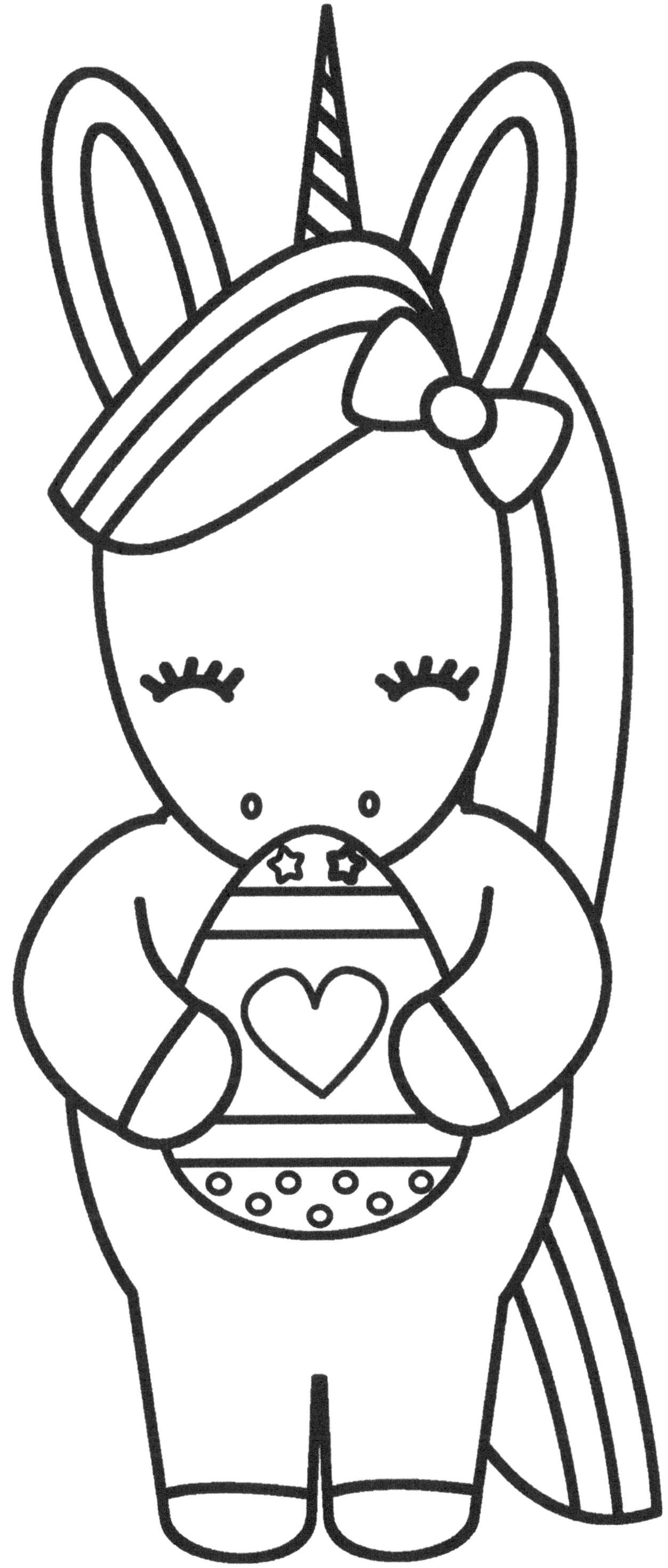

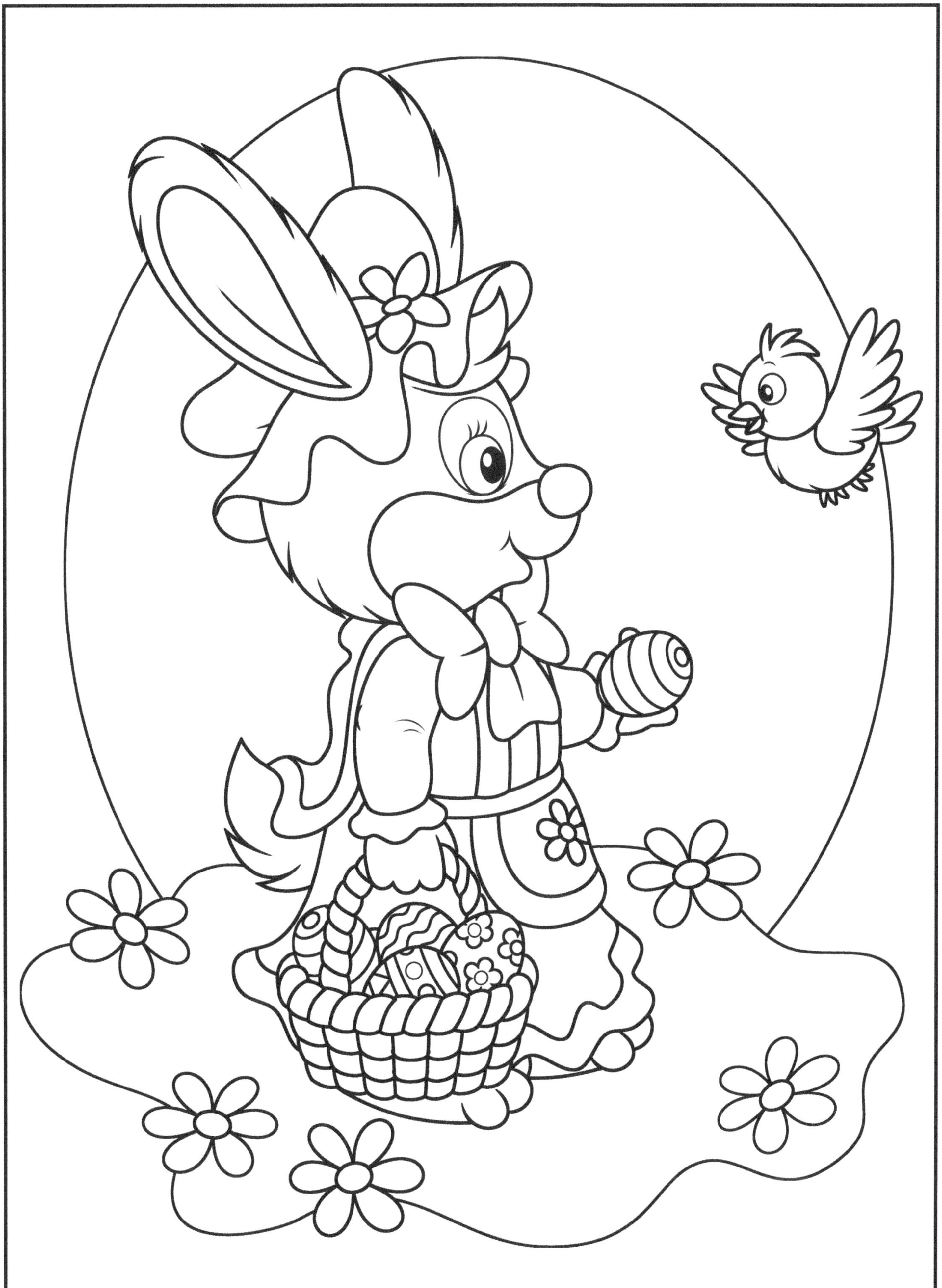

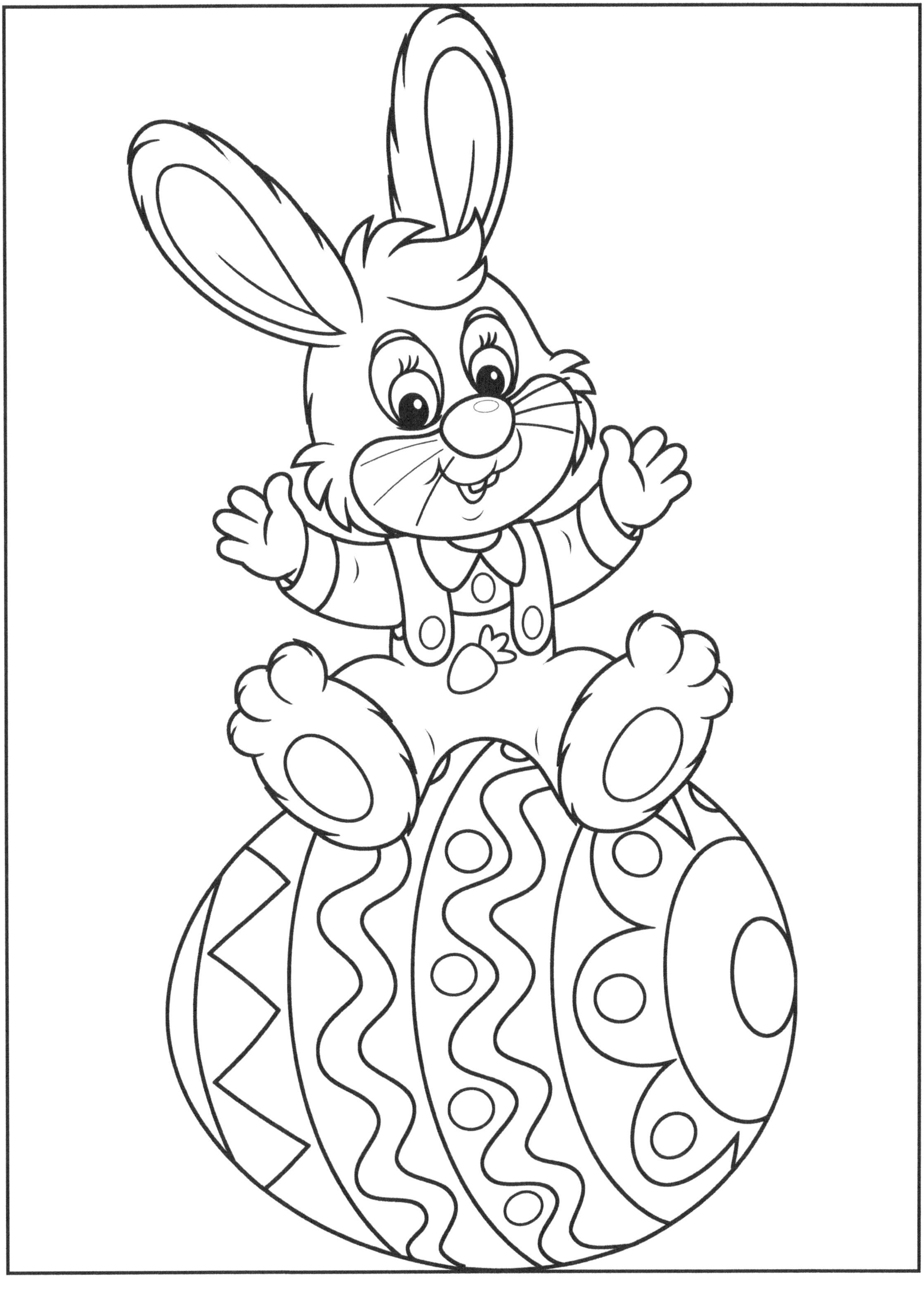

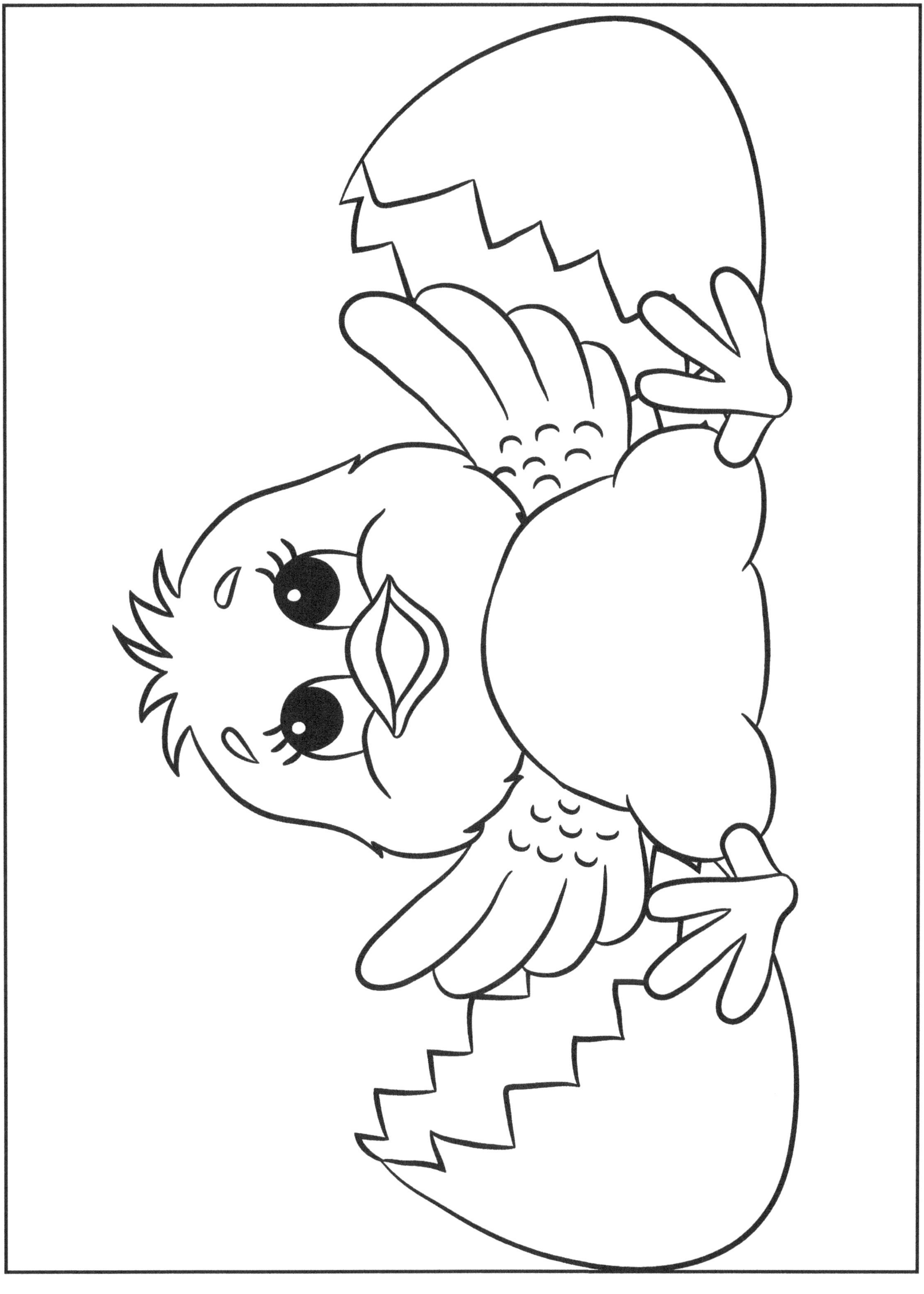

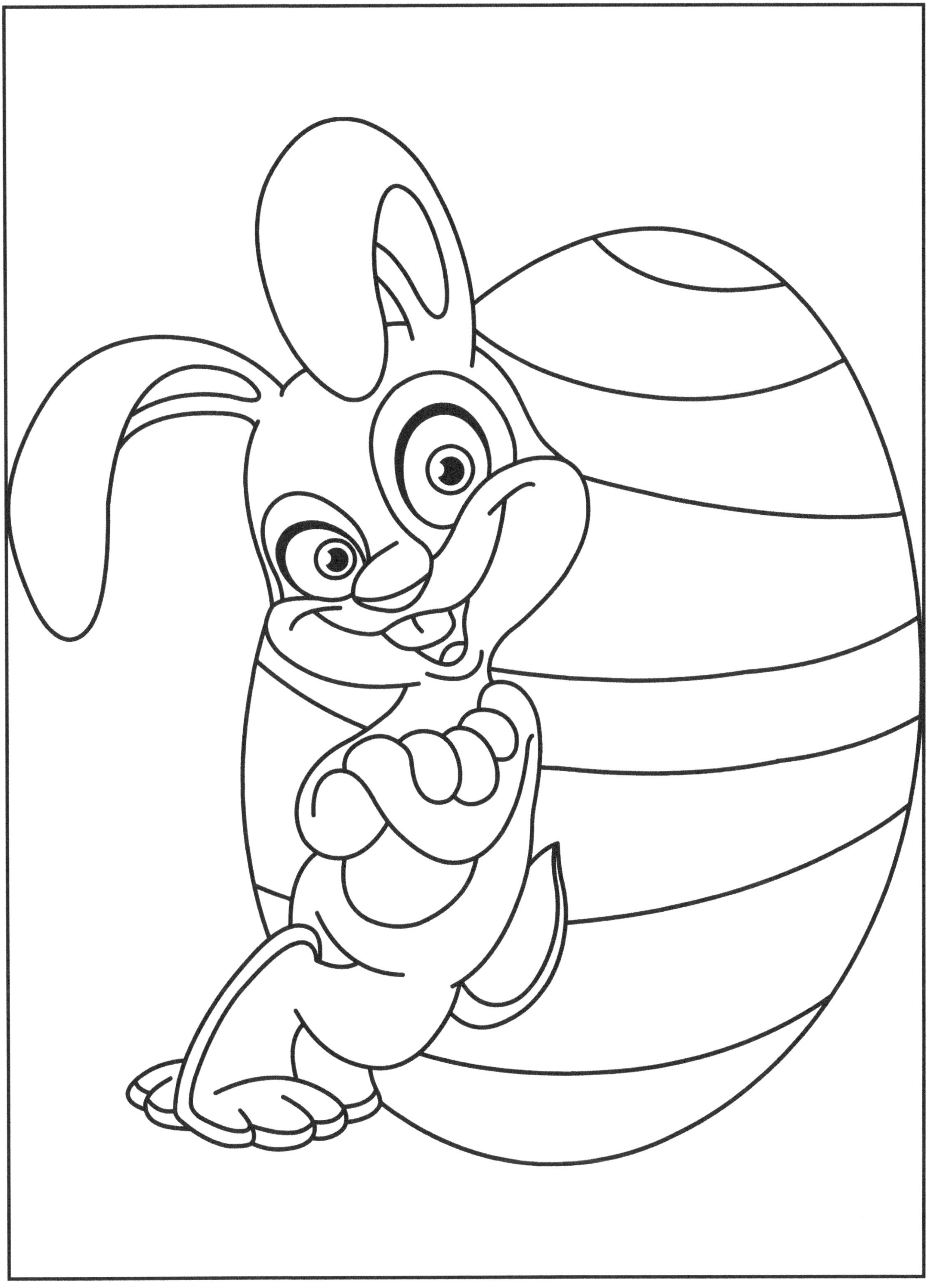

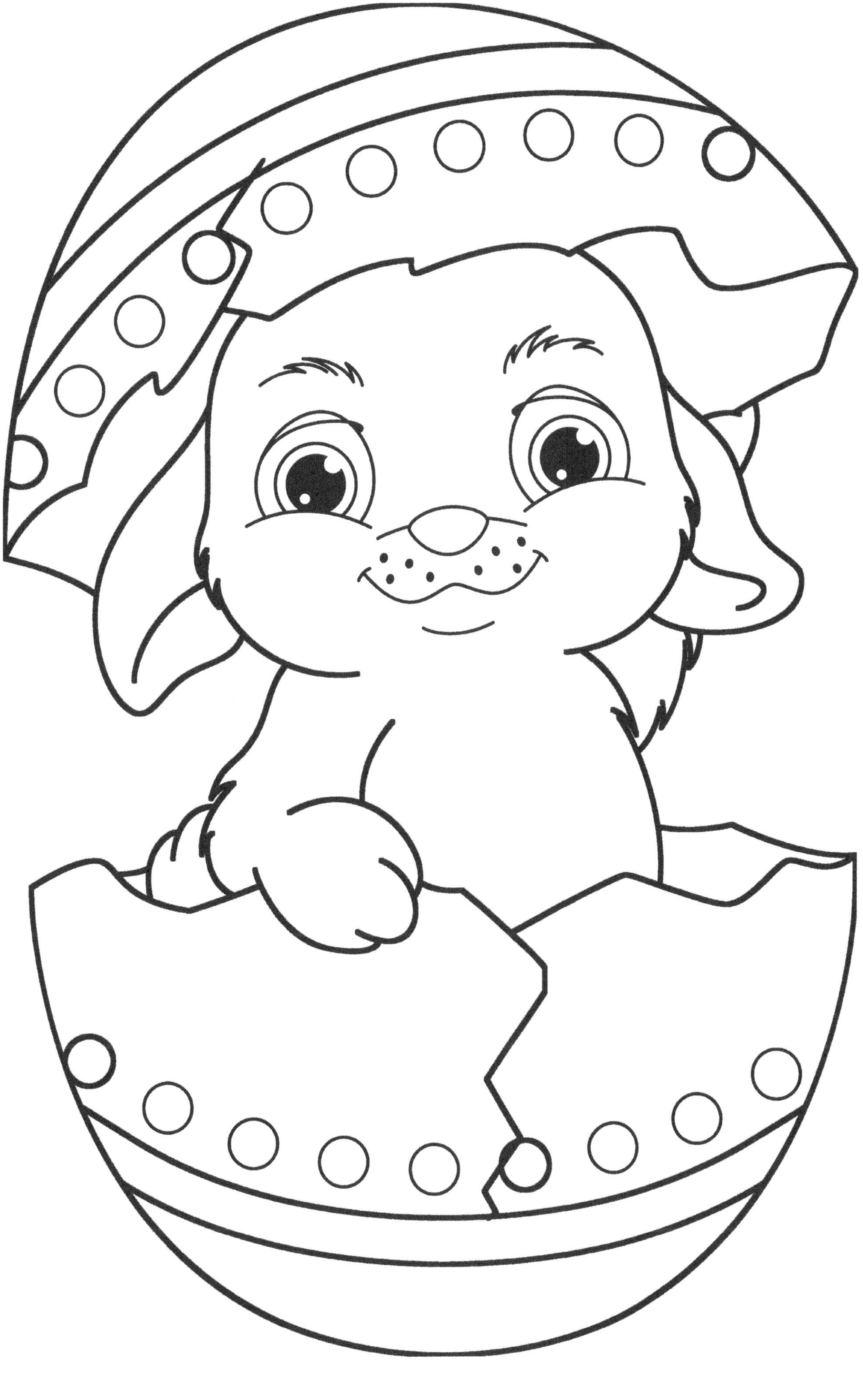

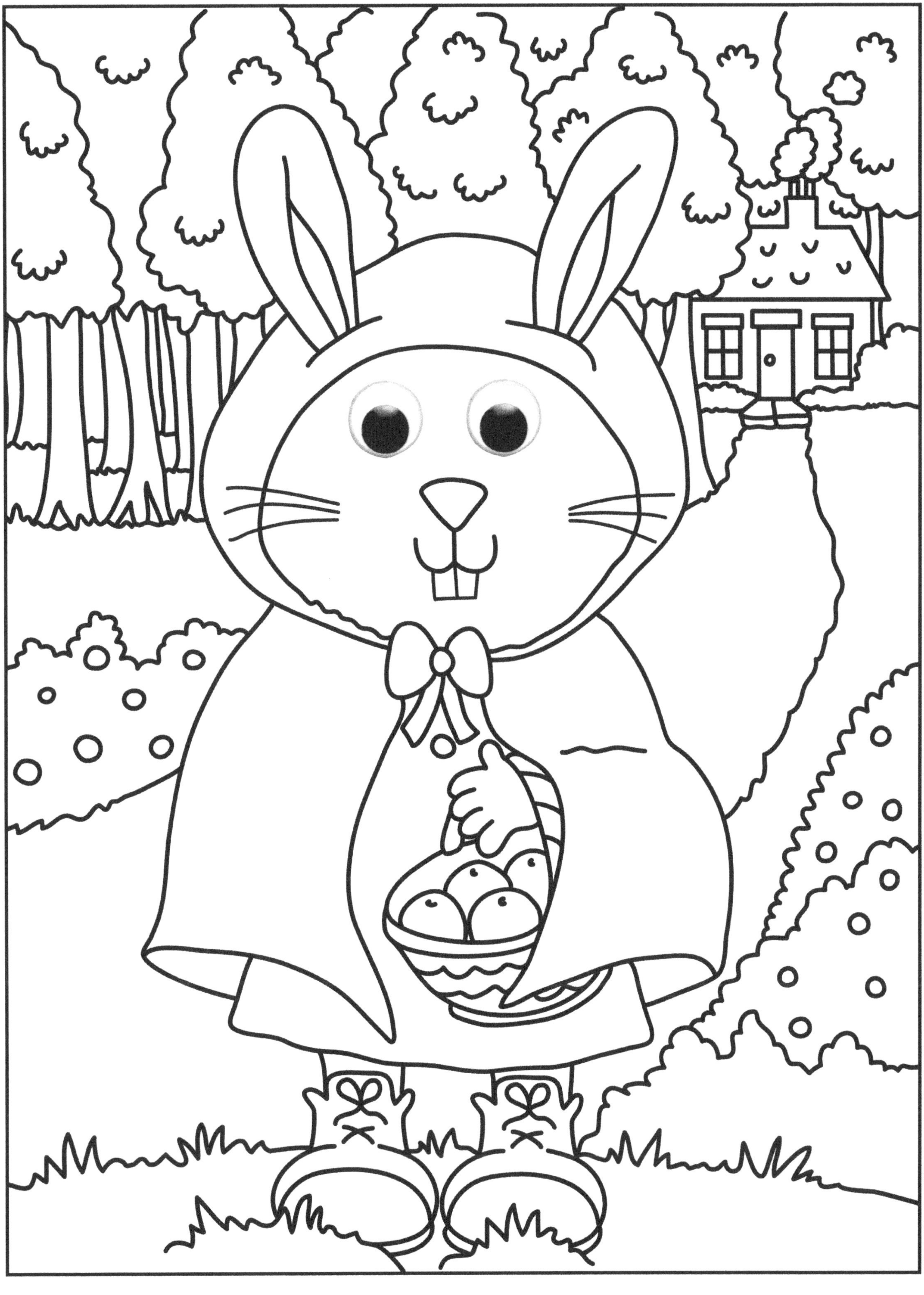

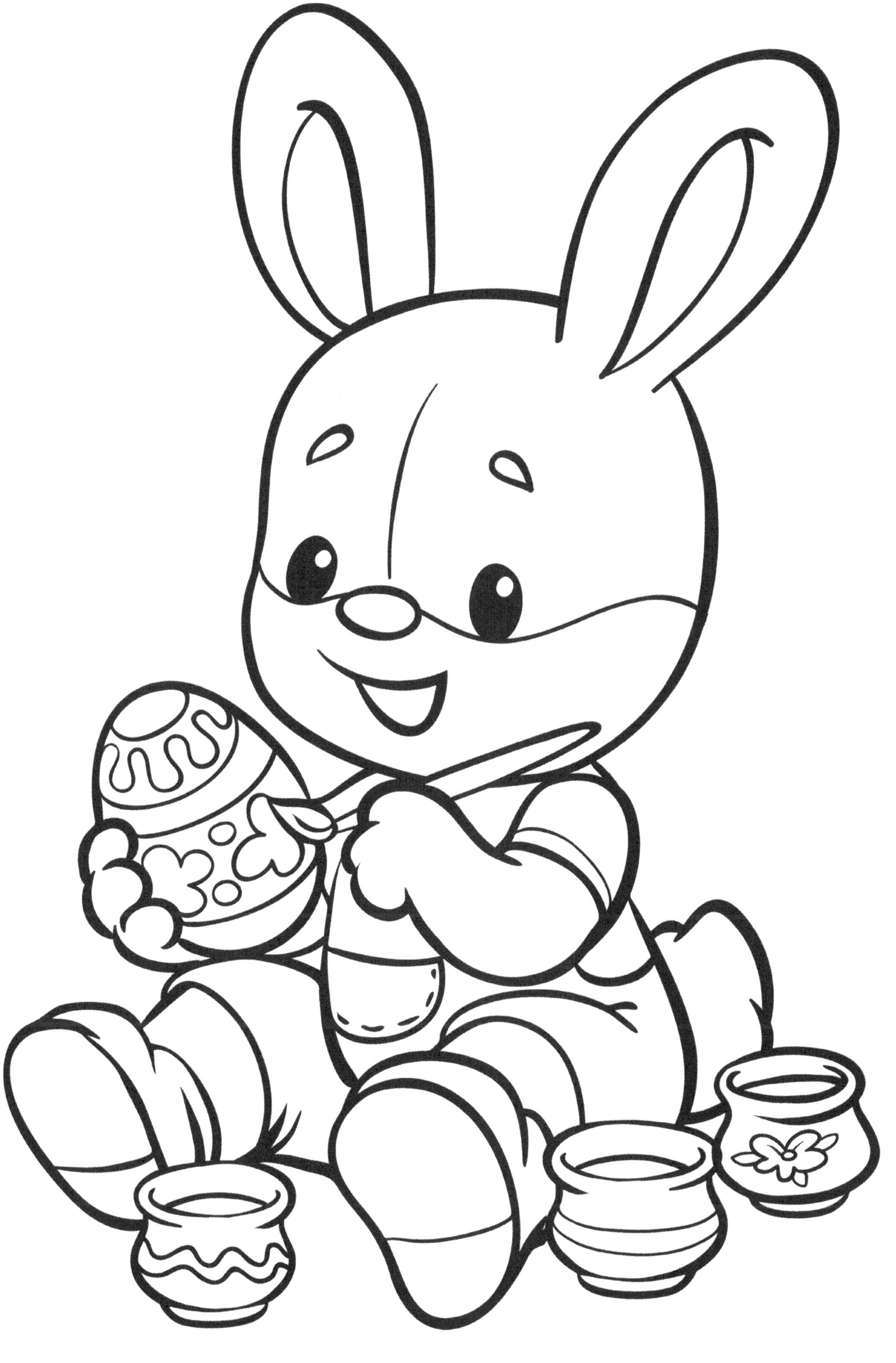

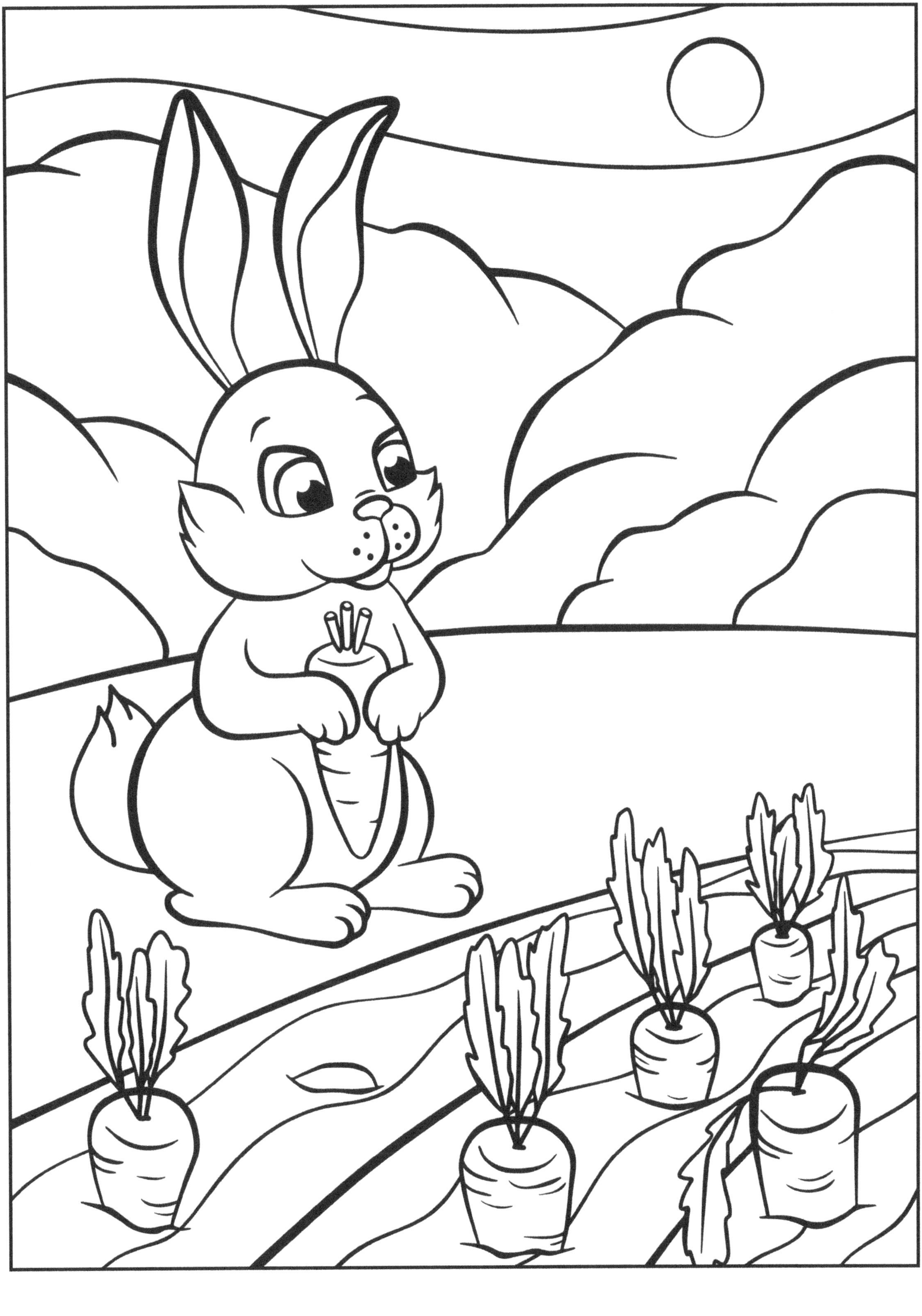

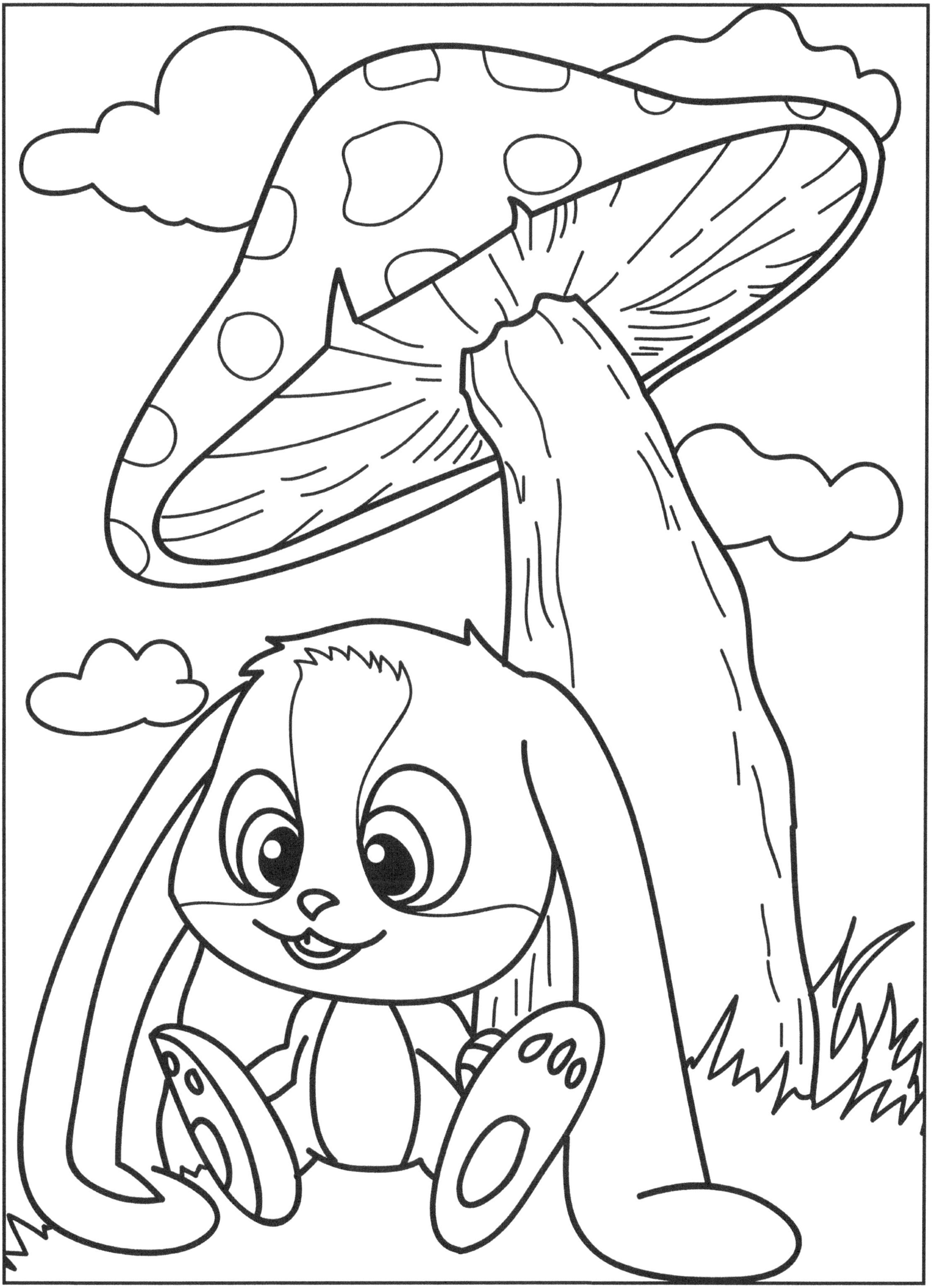

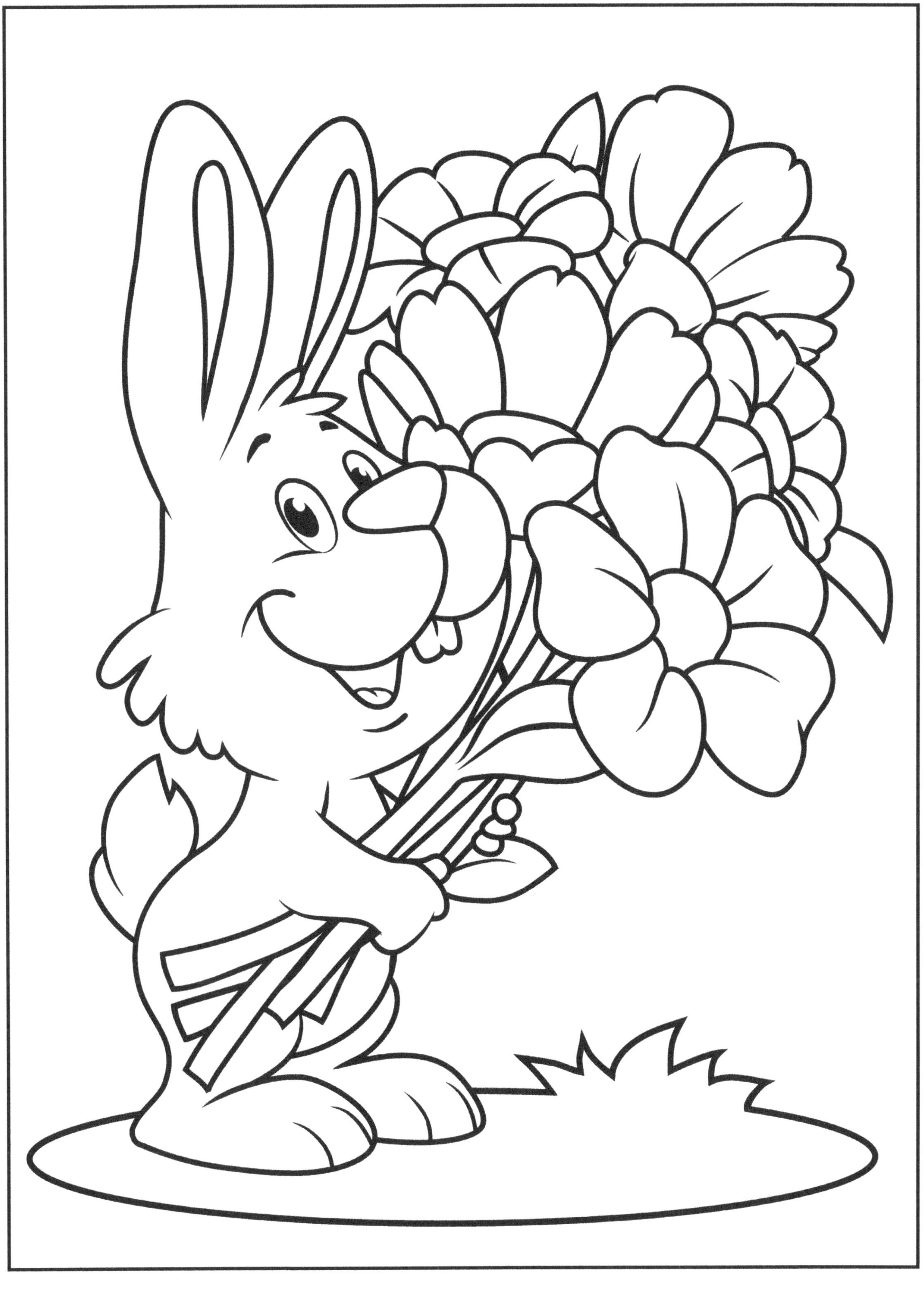

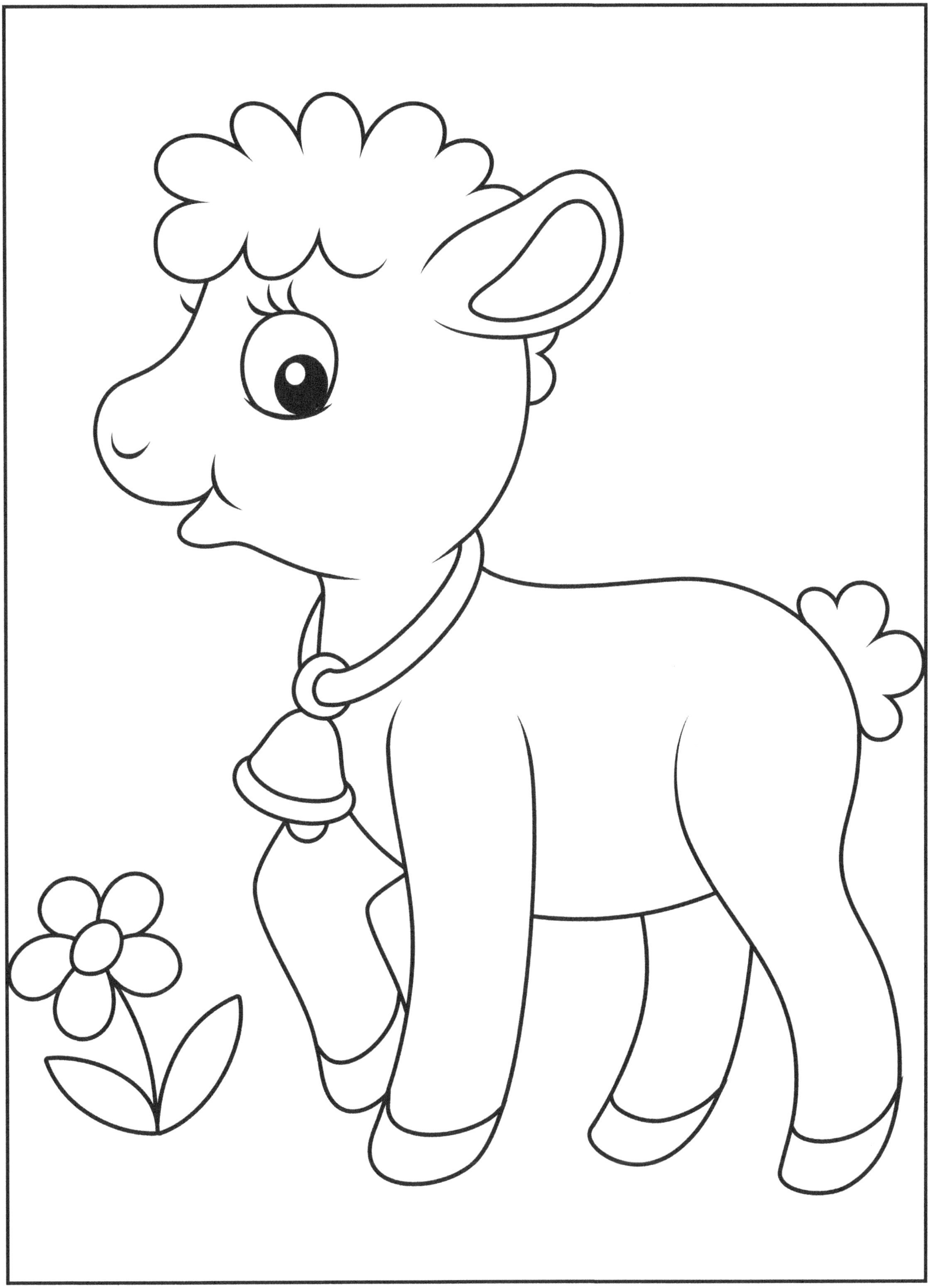

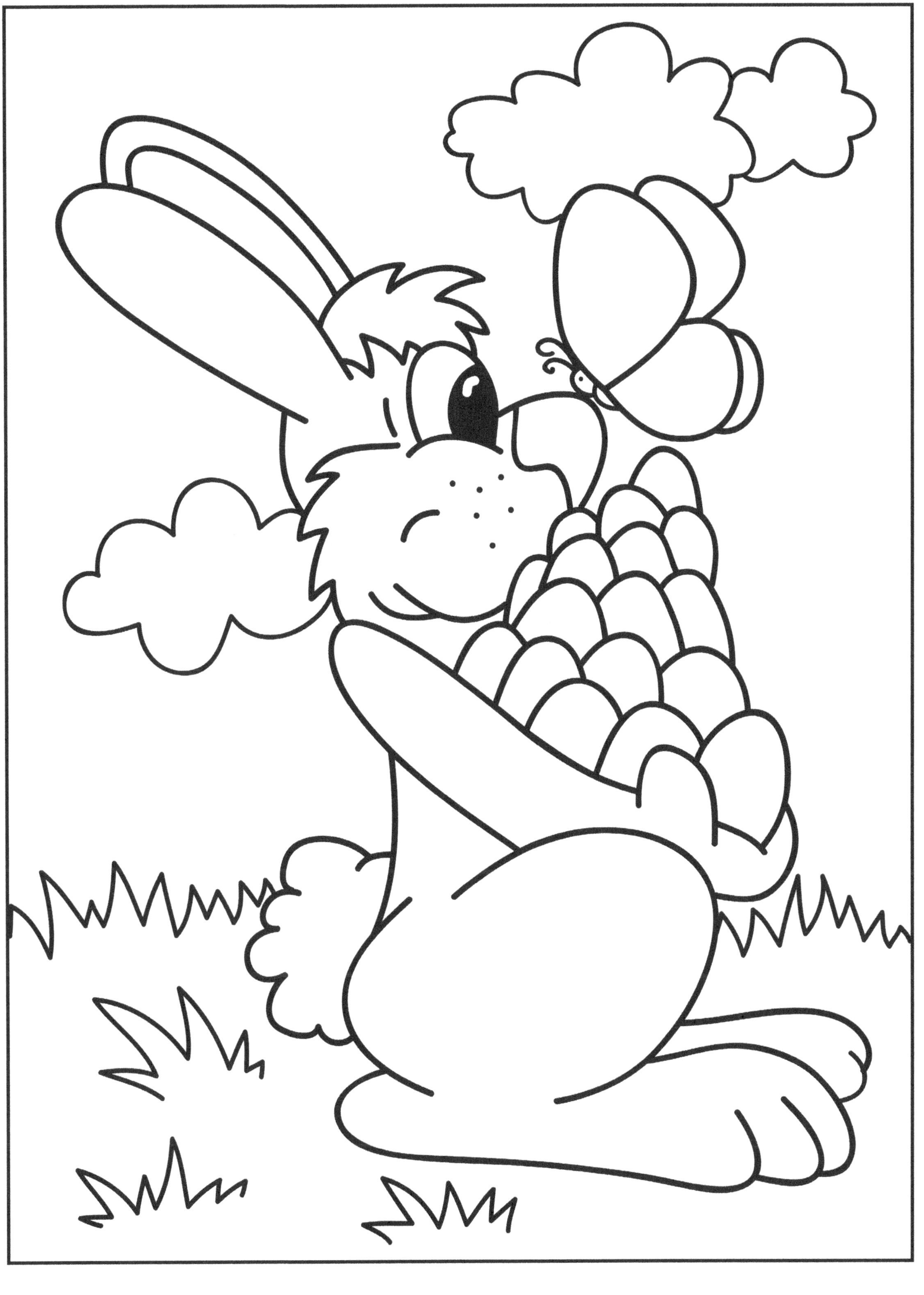

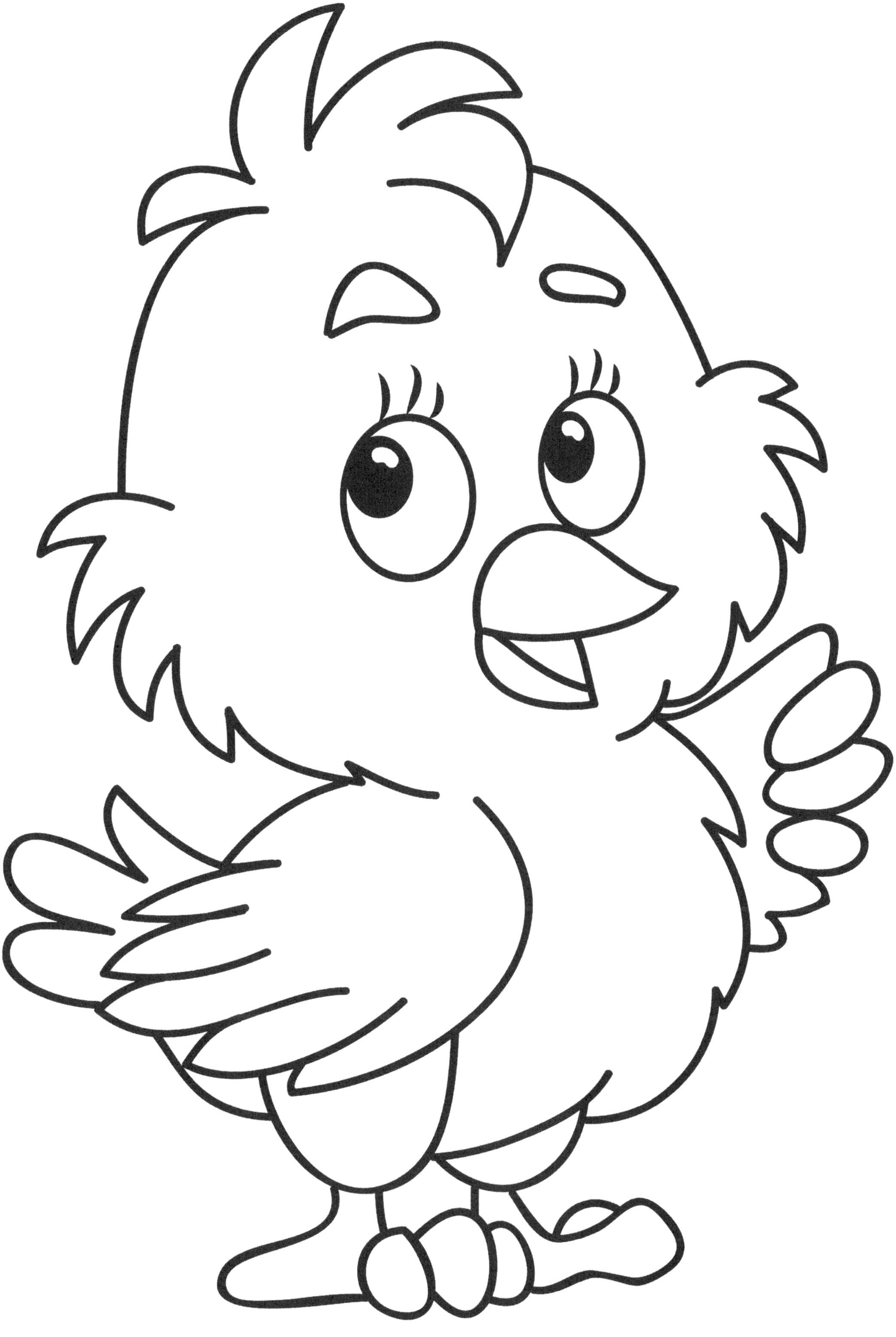

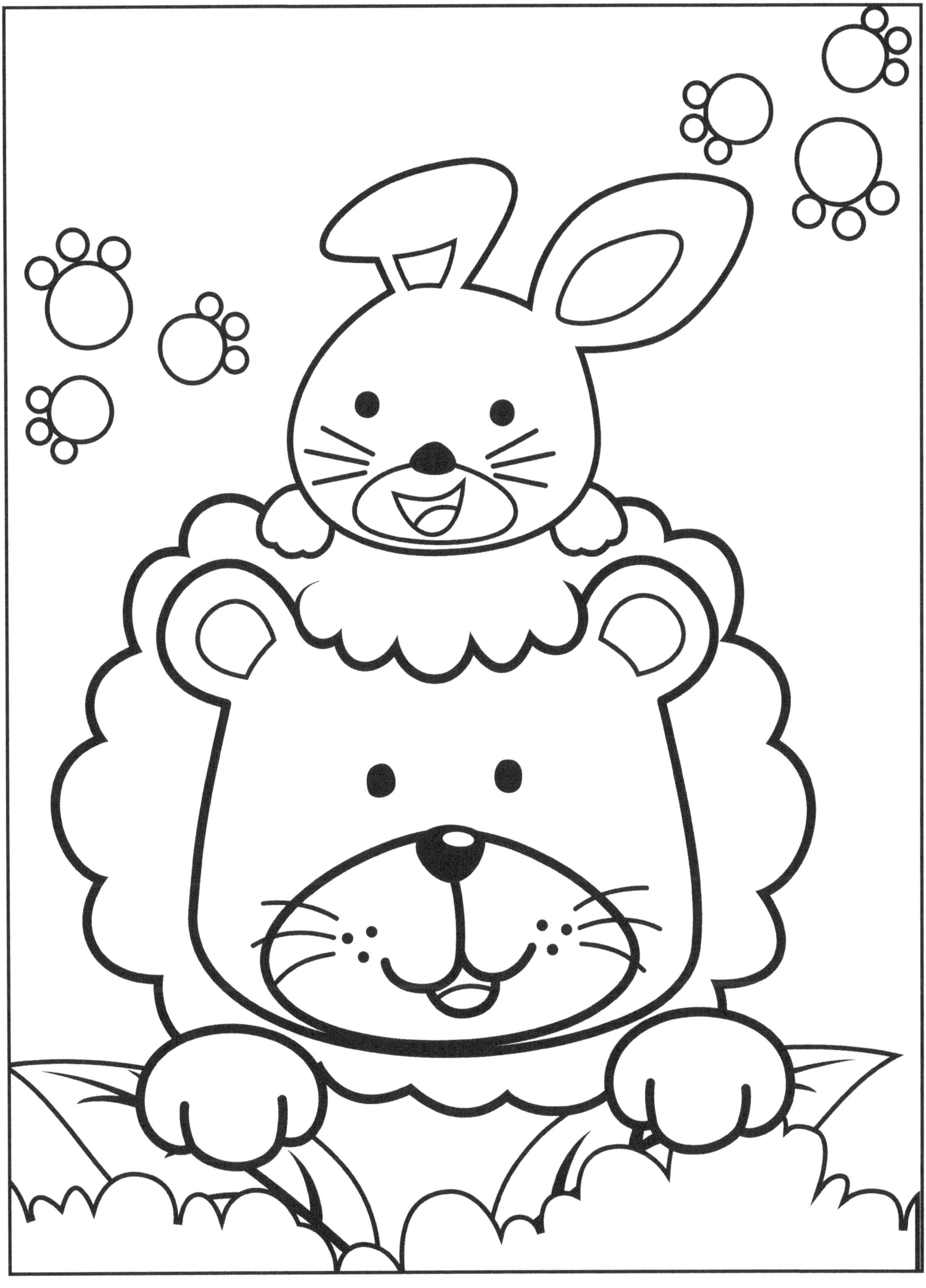

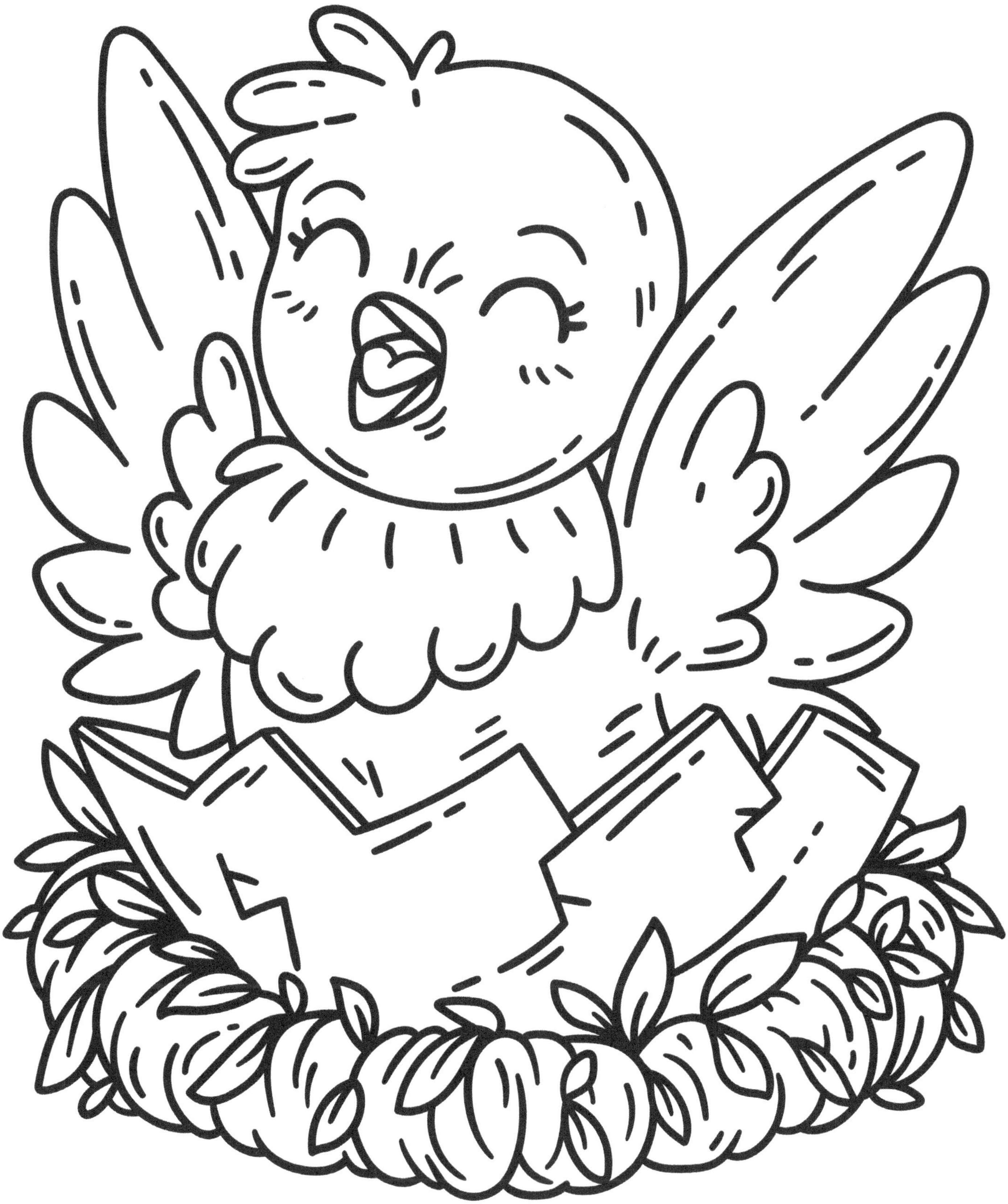

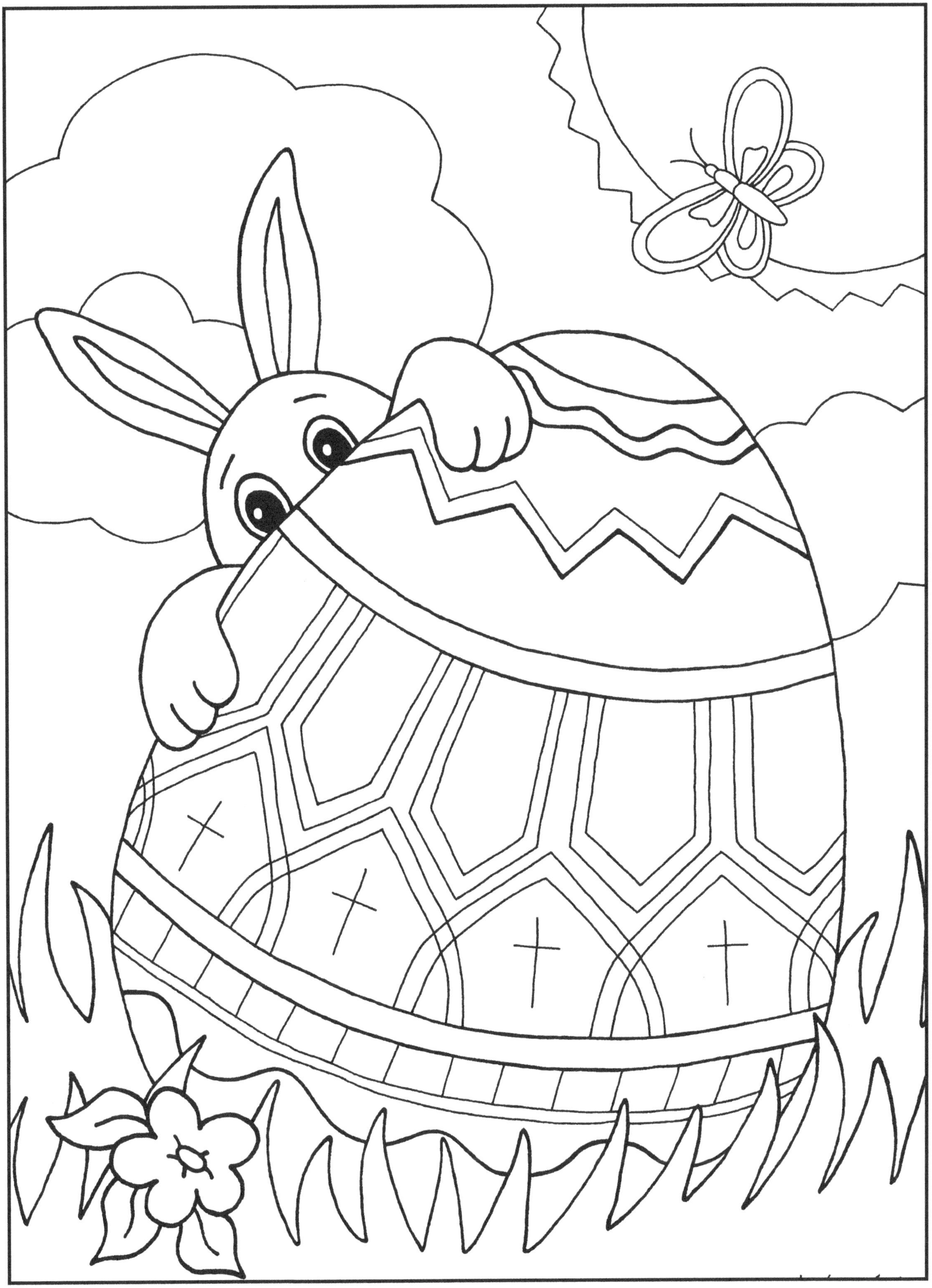

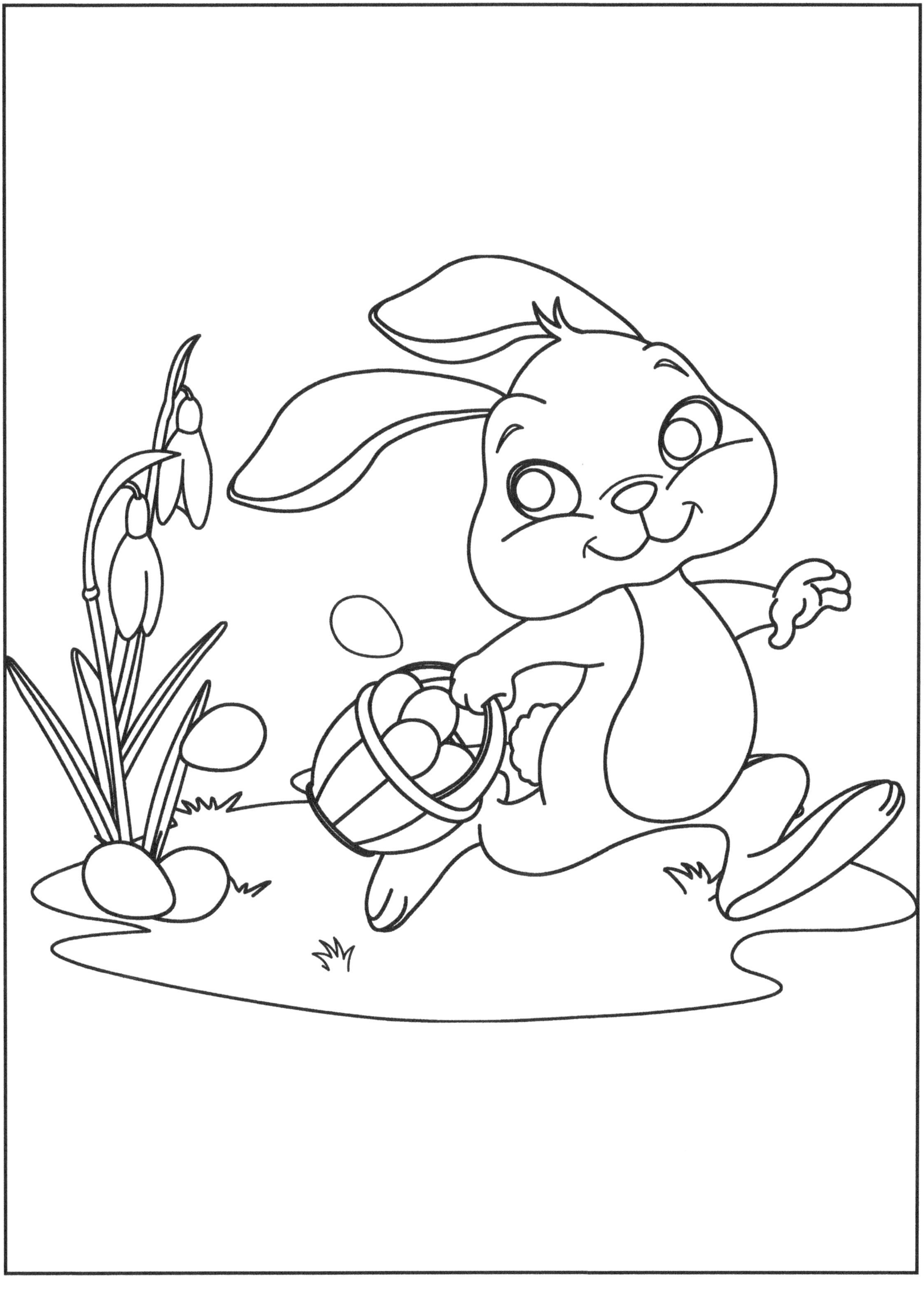

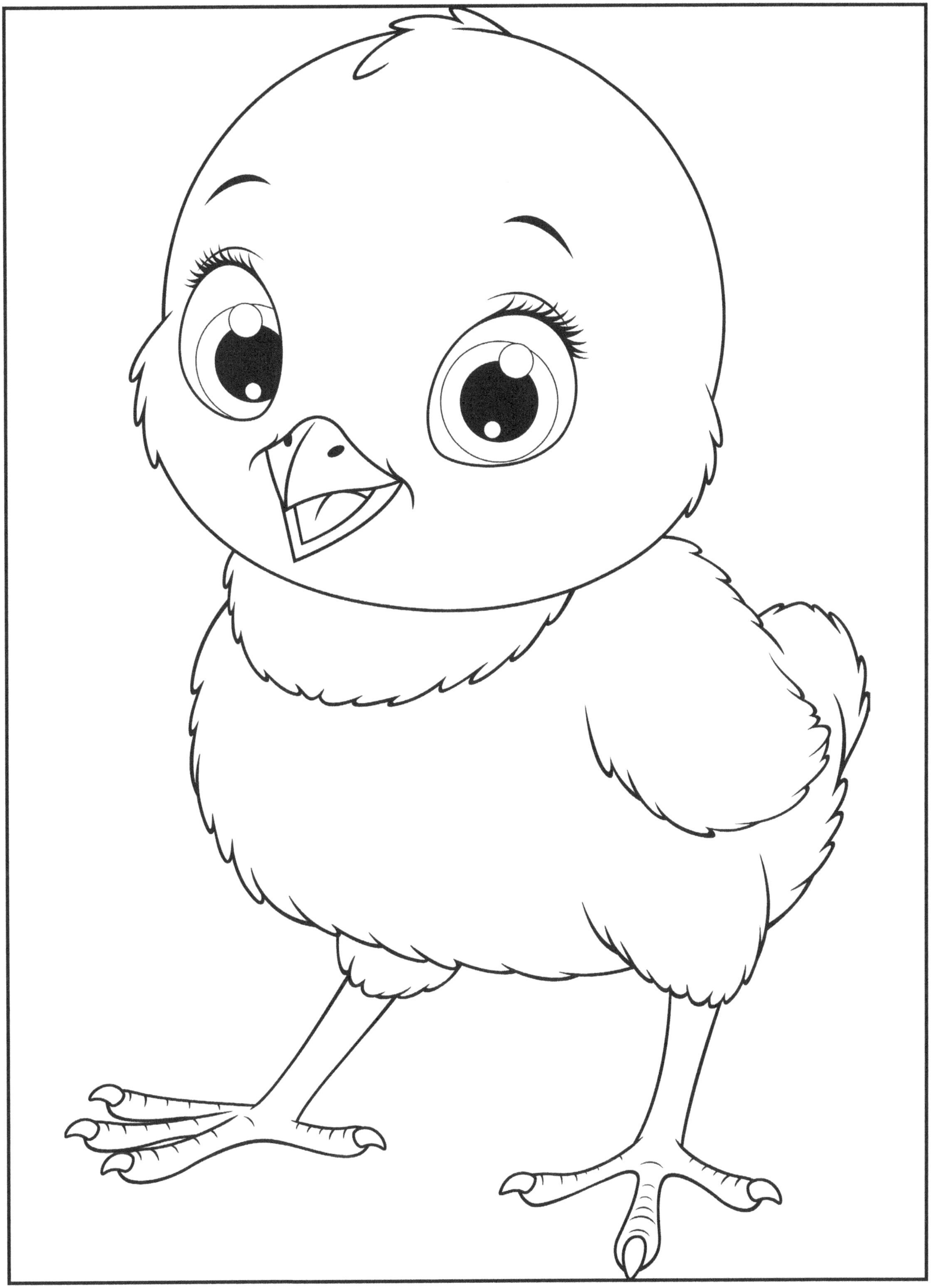

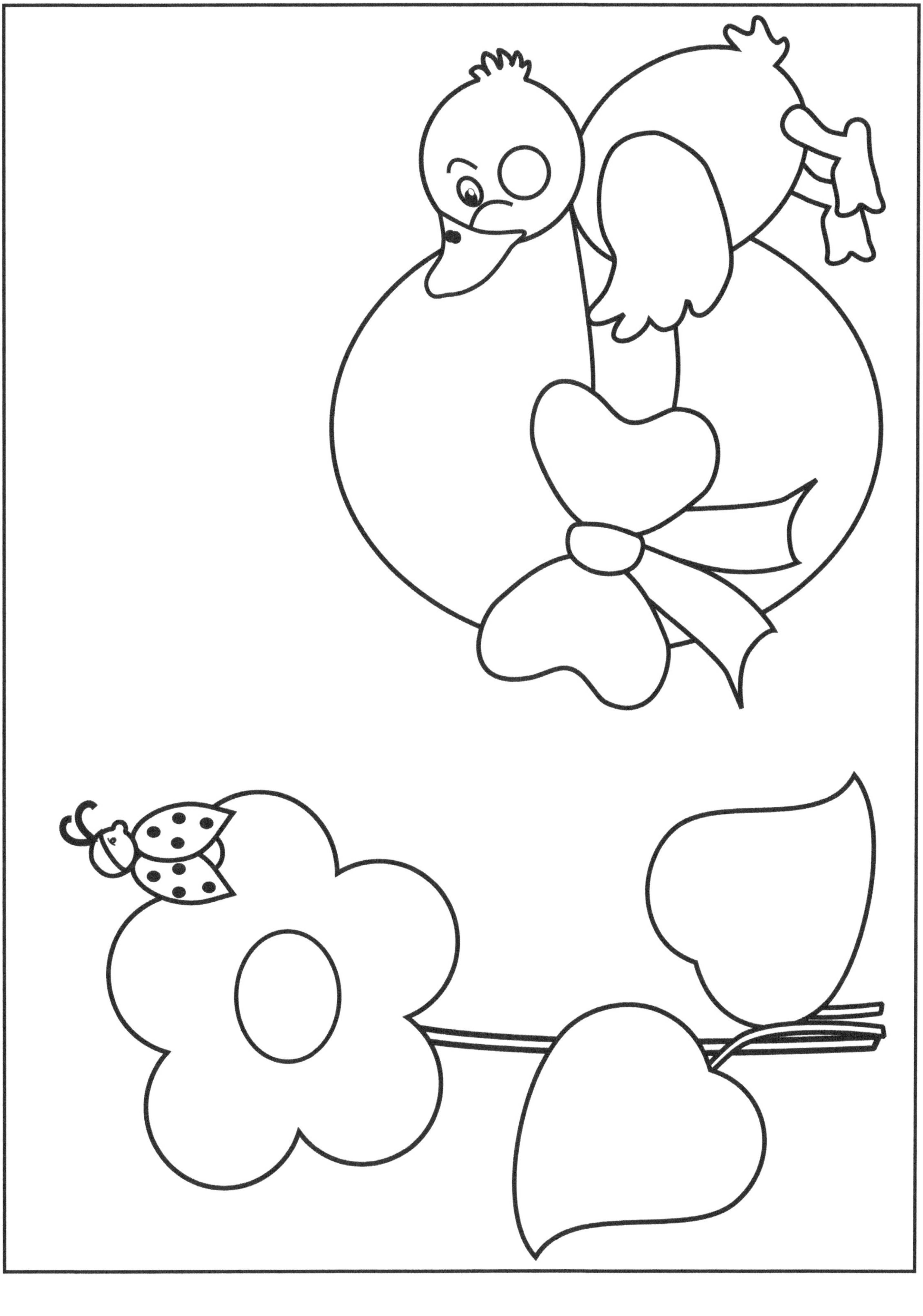

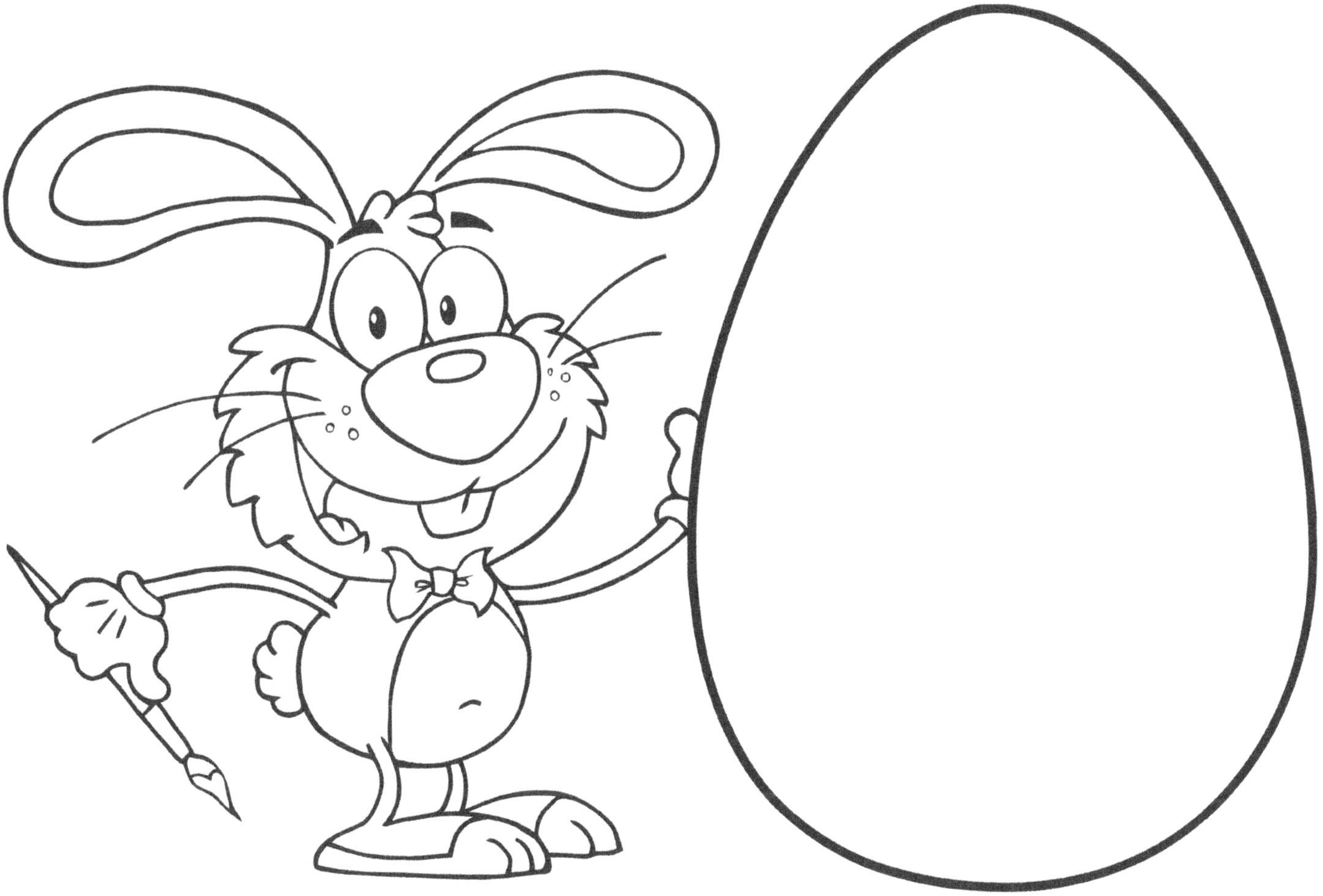

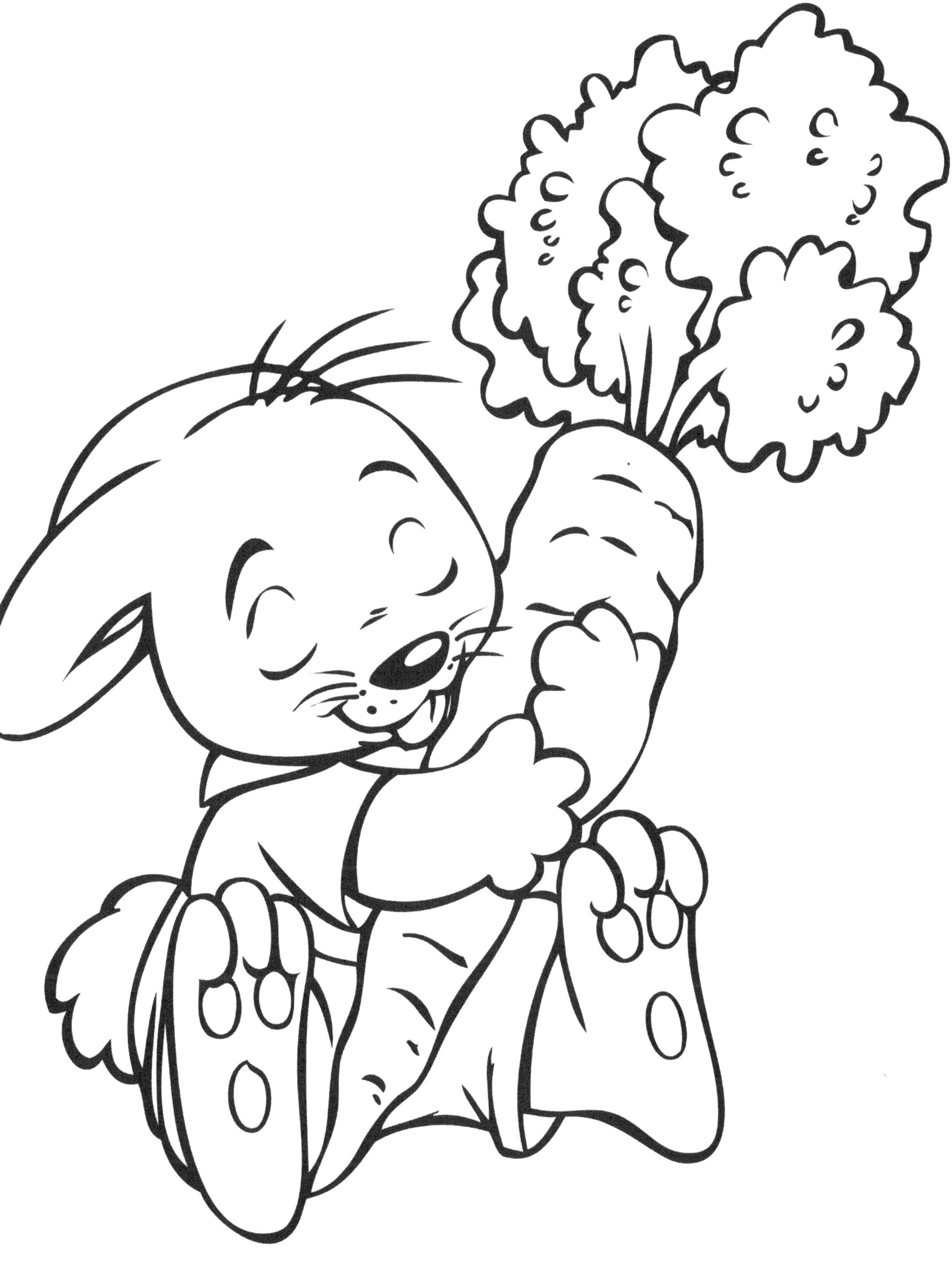

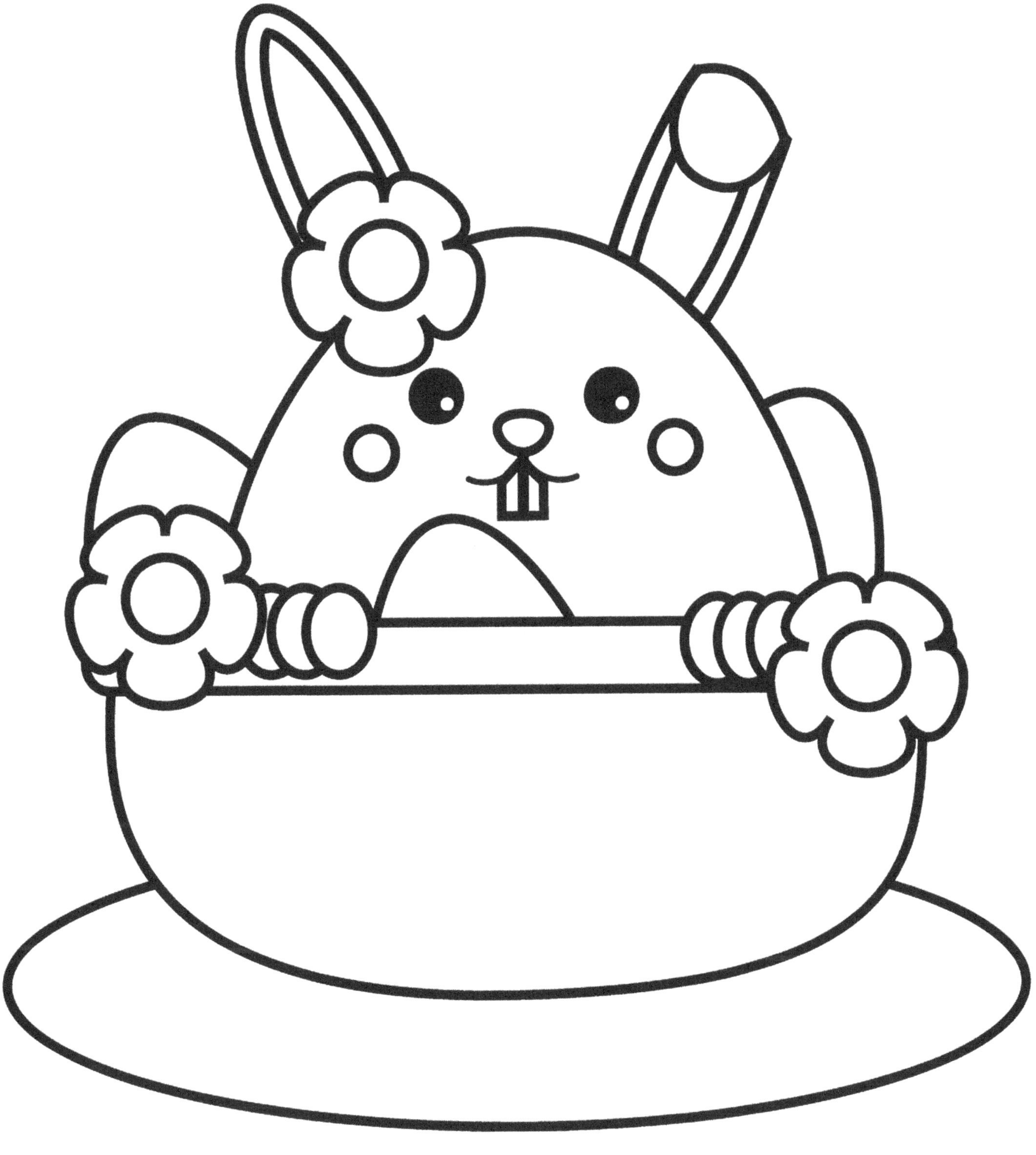

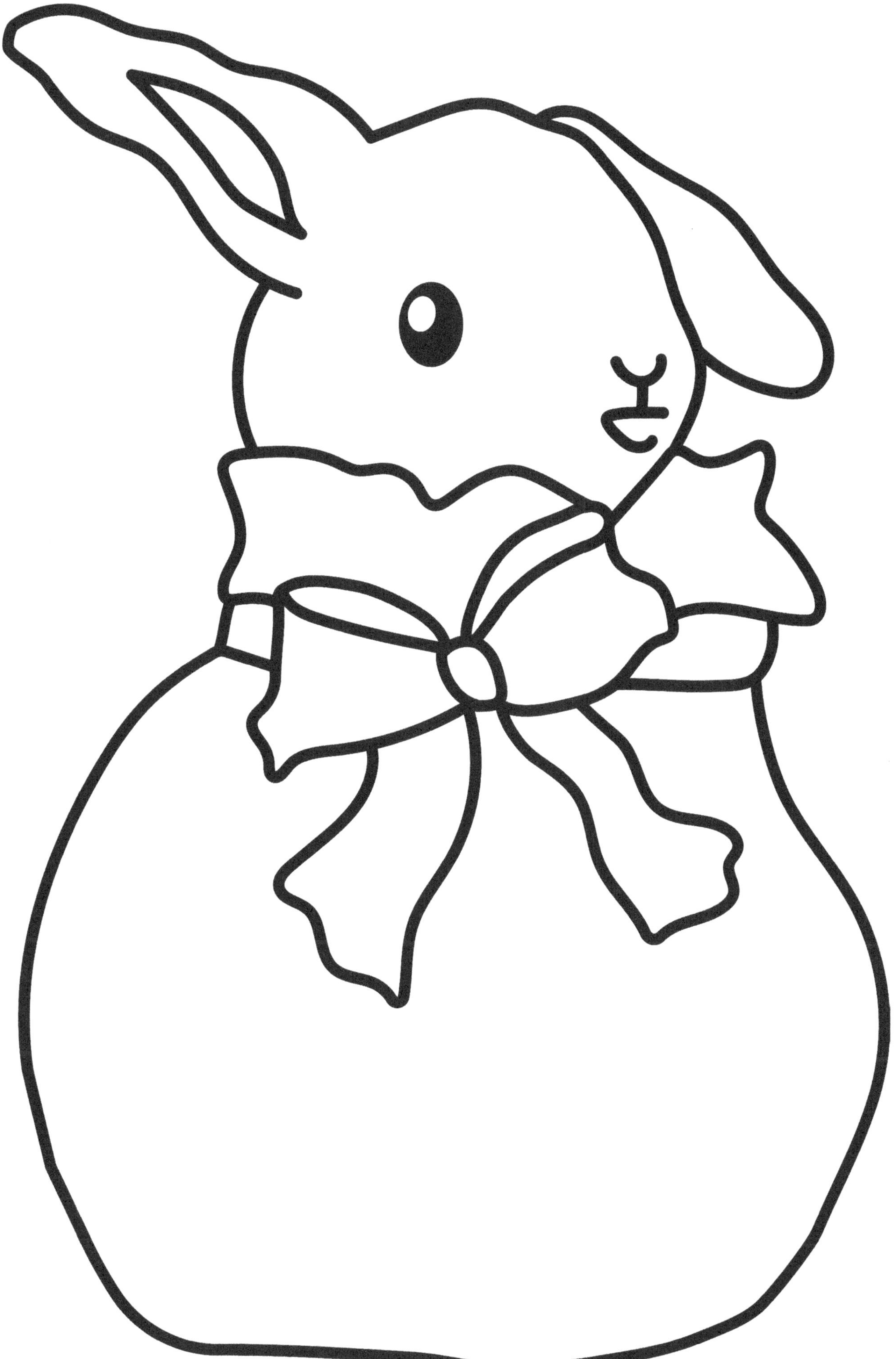